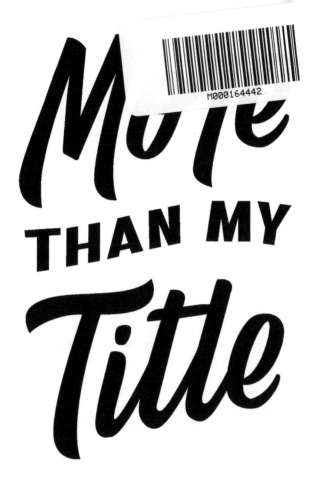

More THAN MY Title

The Power of Hybrid Professionals in a
Workforce of Experts and Generalists

SARABETH BERK, PH.D.

More Than My Title Workbook: Find Your Hybrid Professional
Identity

www.morethanmytitle.com
info@morethanmytitle.com

ISBN 978-1-944027-67-4

Ordering Information:
Quantity sales. Special discounts are available on quantity purchases
by corporations, associations, and others. For details, contact the
publisher at the address above.

Cover Design: Meg Howard

More

THAN MY

Title

ADVANCE PRAISE

"Integrating our career capital in combined identities, to me, seems less like an exception and more like an evolutionary need in the professional realm. Berk is taking the concept one step further. And that is great! Once you are in the multi-identity world, the key is to explore the intersections. That is where the unique value lies. Thank you for contributing to this fascinating space"

—*Rafael Sarandeses, head of financial services at Talengo, executive search and leadership development, executive coach, career fitness professor*

"I had the opportunity to see Sarabeth Berk's presentation at Denver Startup Week, and it changed the way I think about my career and professional persona. The idea of combining professional identities was so new and liberating that I have shared it with all of my friends and family. Since then, I've started the process of merging my various professional identities."

—*Alejandro Silva, digital content and engagement director*

"We are in the fourth industrial revolution, requiring us to be specialists in cross-connection, cross-cultural, and multi-dimensional opportunities. We need X-shaped humans with hybridized skill sets. Hybrids utilize traditional methods while exploring new modes and mindsets to tackle the complexities of our times."

—*David Clifford, serial edu-agitator igniting the creative courage and equity-centered designer in students and educators*

"The thing I love about living this professional hybrid life is the generative space between them."

—*Anne Thulson, artist and teacher, with little distinction between the two*

Dedicated to the icon in my life who truly embodies hybridity and always defies traditional labels, E.G.B.

Ready to be *more* than your job title?

Custom PDF Activities

Online Community

On Demand Video Lessons

Book and Workbook

THE ONLINE COURSE IS NOW AVAILABLE!

Enroll in this 30-day journey to feel more empowered and confident about your work identity to achieve your deepest career dreams. By the end, you'll have a custom hybrid title that captures your uniqueness and competitive advantage.

The course is loaded with:
- 3 hours of video instruction
- Step-by-step guidance along a six-part journey
- A full workbook with powerful activities
- and so much more!

www.morethanmytitle.com

Apply the ideas from this book to your professional life by following the custom activities in the companion workbook.

Available for purchse on Amazon or at
www.morethanmytitle.com

A portion of sales from this book will be donated to
Project Glimmer

Project Glimmer inspires at-risk teenage girls and women to believe in themselves by letting them know their community cares. They host events called Work Your Magic, A Day of Empowerment to bring confidence, inner beauty, and real-life career skills to foster and at-risk girls striving toward graduation.

www.projectglimmer.org

CONTENTS

Preface...xiii

You're Likely a Hybrid Professional if…..xxi

---

01. Discovering Hybrid Professionals   1

1: The Pain Behind the *What Do You Do?* Question 3

2: Are You a Hybrid Professional?..21

3: How Do You Answer What Do You Do?..49

---

02. The Path Toward Hybrid Professional Identity   75

4: Getting Clear on Identity and Professional Identity.......................77

5: Three Types of Identity: Singularity, Multiplicity, Hybridity....87

6: Developing Hybrid Professional Identity...99

7: Investigating the Intersections...117

8: Stories from the Intersections..141

---

03. Preparing for a Future of Hybrid Professionals   157

9: Recruiting, Hiring, and Managing Hybrid Professionals..........159

10: The Future Is Definitely Hybrid...179

A Free Instructional Guide To Help You Find Your Hybrid Professional Identity...191

Acknowledgments...193

Bibliography...195

About the Author...205

PREFACE

*"The era of doing just one thing is over. So go ahead and
embrace your writer/entrepreneur/banjo player title—it
makes you more interesting and adaptable."*
— ***Jessica Stillman, @EntryLevelRebel***

THIS BOOK IS FOR professionals who wear many hats but struggle to explain how all those hats fit together. When the world doesn't fully appreciate your professional value, how can you communicate it better? This question gets at professional identity—the identities we use in our work. Many of us have more than one professional identity, and are both experts and generalists at the same time.

This book is about integrating our multiple professional identities and why that matters. We've never been told we're allowed to blend identities, and we don't know how to explain that this is what makes us unique. Integration, instead of separation, of professional identities is a critical distinction in how we work. Many of us are multi-*something*: multitalented, multihyphenate, multipassionate, multidisciplinary, or multidimensional. As *hybrid professionals,* we have a combination of competencies and more than one identity simultaneously. The concept of the hybrid professional empowers us to own all of our identities and be our fullest professional selves.

As hybrid professionals, we need to learn how to articulate our hybridity and advocate for hybrid roles. The responsibility of spreading this term falls on us as much as it does on leaders, clients, managers, and colleagues. Employers and clients need to understand how to work with us so we can thrive. Otherwise, we wither in roles that force us to inhabit only one of our professional identities at a time.

Hybrid professional identity is critical to the evolution of the workforce. It's been a hidden phenomenon for too long. If you didn't realize you're a hybrid professional, things are about to change. It's here! Start calling yourself a hybrid professional.

Purpose of This Book

The overarching goal of this book is to showcase the power of the hybrid professional identity and its important role in the workforce. This book discusses hybrid professionals—the value we bring, who we are, what defines us, and what happens when we cross our different professional identities. If you're a professional who feels like a square peg in a round hole, who has expertise in more than one discipline, who juggles unrelated career interests, or who is seen as someone who transitions between jobs too often, then this book is for you.

The reason this book matters is because the workforce is undergoing rapid transformation. Hybrid professionals are already shifting work culture, hiring practices, and other management processes, but we're not being recognized. Nor are hybrids widely discussed in business strategy, job markets, or hiring practices. Why is this?

The world demands hybrid professional identities today and will continue to in the future. Traditional job titles and careers are being upended right before our very eyes. Linear career paths and hierarchical corporate structures are shifting beneath us. As the world becomes a more complex, volatile, and unpredictable place, it impacts the way we develop, grow, and make decisions around our careers and professional identity.

The two questions I'm asked most often are *Who are hybrids?* and *What does hybridity look like?* That's what this book will answer.

Overview of This Book

This book isn't a career guide or a work style assessment. It's aimed at helping you unpack and reframe your professional identity, especially if you think of yourself as a jack-of-all-trades. This book is partially about professional identity and branding, and partially a new framework for thinking about professionals. In each chapter, you'll learn more about what hybrid professional identity means, what it looks like, and how to define your hybridity. At the end of each chapter, ideas are summarized in a section called "Key Ideas About Hybrid Professionals."

Part One explores the struggle that hybrid professionals experience and what hybridity looks like in the workforce. There's an analysis of that pesky question of *what do you do?* and an explanation of why we're having professional identity crises. You'll read stories about hybrids, from famous to everyday, to illustrate what makes them who they are. And my personal journey of how I began this research and discovered I'm a hybrid is woven throughout.

Part Two focuses on definitions and the framework behind hybrid professional identity. This includes a review of research on identity and identity studies before moving into key aspects of what hybridity means, and how a person evolves into it. Since the intersections of professional identities are a critical element of hybridity, there's an entire chapter on that. Examining hybridity is a reflective journey, and you'll see why in this section.

Part Three examines the hybrid professional from the perspective of the employer and the job market. It also gives a glimpse into the future of work. You'll learn what employers and recruiters should know about hybrids. There are important details to consider and questions to ask when recruiting, hiring, training, and retaining hybrids. The final chapter looks at how the future is hybrid and what that means as society continues to transform.

By the end of this book, you will:

- Understand three types of professional identity: singularity, multiplicity, and hybridity.

- See the value of hybrid professionals and why the term needs to be popularized in the workforce.
- Feel permission to be a hybrid professional if you think you are one.
- Have tools and resources to discover your hybrid professional identity so you can articulate what you do.

Who Should Read This Book

Hybrid professionals: Do employers or clients struggle to understand you and what you can do? Or are you stuck in a box and know you're more than your title? If you can't deliver a crystal-clear, ten-second explanation of your professional identity because it's too complicated or you wear too many hats, then keep reading. By the end of this book, you'll have insights around how to succinctly articulate your hybridity. You'll understand how to harness your hybridity as a professional asset, and be more aware of what makes you a hybrid so you're more confident about sharing it.

Business leaders and managers: This book will help you realize there are three types of workers in the workforce, those with singular, multiple, and hybrid professional identities. All three types are necessary, but for different reasons. If you're looking for people who bring a competitive advantage and innovative thinking or abilities to their work, you may have been overlooking hybrids. Knowing why hybrid professionals are important for your organization and what makes them tick will help you execute on your mission and make you more successful at keeping this talent.

Recruiters: This book will build your awareness of hybrid professionals, why they're valuable employees, and what to consider during recruitment. You'll gain tips on how to discern them in a pool of candidates. It will also give you suggestions on specific questions to use during recruiting and why those questions matter.

Human resources professionals: This book will help you understand that when hybrid professionals are hired, they may become frustrated by internal operating systems and processes. Hybrids require fluidity in their roles and reporting structures. They test a company's policies if they're too rigid and conditional. You'll learn what to expect when hybrid professionals are part of your workplace.

Career advisors: This book will provide guidance around how to frame professional identity and break stereotypes around being an expert or a generalist. You'll learn specific tips and questions to ask advisees who are sorting through multiple career interests. Instead of focusing on what someone is passionate about and the purpose they want to serve in the world, you'll learn to open discussion around identity and the multiple identities a worker possesses. The aspect of identity, in addition to passion and purpose, should be the third leg of a three-legged stool in career conversations.

An Instructional Guide to Help You Find Your Hybrid Professional Identity

While this book focuses on defining hybrid professional identity and what hybrids look like in the workforce, the question of how to discover your hybrid professional identity is also very important. I want to help you apply this content to yourself. Skip to the end for a free, five-step instructional guide on how to find your hybrid professional identity. You'll find this guide valuable if you don't know your hybrid professional identity or want to sharpen it.

YOU'RE LIKELY A HYBRID PROFESSIONAL IF...

IF YOU THINK YOU'RE a hybrid professional, or just want to learn more about hybrids, the following statements will help you do a quick self-check:

- You struggle to express what you do. You're good at a lot of things, but you can't distill your professional identity down to its core essence. You need help to figure out how to explain your professional value.
- You are "everything." You wear multiple hats for work. You have multiple job titles or even multiple business cards and websites. Your LinkedIn profile has a list of identities in the header of your profile.
- Nobody knows what you do. Your aunt, your mom, your best friend, your neighbor can't fully describe what you do. People are confused about what you do.
- You compartmentalize your professional identities. You're afraid to share or show your multiple professional identities all at once because you think people won't understand how they all fit together. You're tired of the tap dance where you can only use one identity at a time.

- You need to (re)define your professional brand. You aren't sure what to call yourself. You've been using buzzwords or generic language. You're ready to stand out.

If any of these statements ring true for you, then keep reading. You're likely a hybrid professional, and it's time to learn what that means.

PART ONE

Discovering Hybrid Professionals

CHAPTER 1

The Pain Behind the *What Do You Do?* Question

"Why do one thing when you can do two? One discipline illuminates another!"

—Cynthia Weiss, arts education consultant, artist, and educator

"NOBODY KNOWS WHAT I do!" lamented Shawn.[1] "And, the things people know me for aren't the roles I want to get paid for. I'm tired of doing event management, strategic planning, and accounting. I know I'm a good accountant, but it's not what I want to do. I'm clear on what I don't want to do. How do I get people to see me for my other professional identities?"

When I met Shawn for coffee, this was how our conversation started. She had every right to be upset that her career

---

1   Actual names have been changed unless the person's full name and title appears.

wasn't what she wanted it to be. She was tired of being put in a box and only being seen as one type of professional.

Shawn wasn't the first person who voiced these hardships to me. Many people who are multitalented professionals and are great at doing a lot of things for work feel stuck, bored, isolated, and undervalued. After enough time feeling this way, they become frustrated with their careers. They can't figure out where they belong, and they don't know how to be seen for their full range of professional identities.

To make matters worse, employers and clients don't understand what to do with hybrid professionals or that hybrid professionals even exist. They hire them for only one of their strengths, which is why hybrids feel unsatisfied in that role. Or, they mistake their erratic job history, typically a nonlinear career path, as a sign of being a scattered, noncommittal, unspecialized, or unreliable job seeker. In reality, job hopping is a symptom of a hybrid professional who hasn't learned how to showcase their hybridity as an asset. As a result, hybrids keep seeking opportunities where their hybridity can be valued and applied.

> "A hybrid professional is a worker who integrates multiple professional identities together, working from the intersections of those identities."

Ultimately, this process backfires on both sides. Professionals like Shawn can't figure out how to be seen for their professional worth, and they have a lot of it. Hybrids possess rare and valuable skills accumulated from the combination of their various identities. Employers and clients are nervous to work with or hire people like Shawn because they can't understand or fully appreciate the unique value they add. Shawn's background and talents make little sense in traditional work situations, hiring practices, or companies that emphasize linear career pathways, deep expertise, and employees looking to grow into senior positions. It's a tough situation.

The workplace is stuck in a paradigm biased toward hyperspecialization when the world is moving toward hybridization. Businesses want workers who are hyperfocused. But, in a 2019 study published in the *Strategic Management Journal*, Frank Nagle and Florenta Teodoridis found that generalists end up having more impact, appearing in more journals, and receiving more citations by their peers. Nagle and Teodoridis studied researchers who were highly diversified in their disciplinary thinking and practices compared to those who were less diversified.

The argument can be made that businesses benefit from hybrids because they have depth and breadth of knowledge across more than one area. In "The Business Case for Becoming a Jack-of-All-Trades," Michael Blanding writes, "We may be a long way from the Renaissance, but when it comes to novel developments, there still might be some value in being a Renaissance man or woman."

Shawn's predicament wasn't unique. But she felt like it was. Shawn was struggling to be seen in the workplace and to be fairly compensated for the multiple hats she wore. She didn't realize she was a hybrid, or that that required her to market and brand herself differently than an expert or a generalist. This is a problem facing many workers today.

When I started this journey, I thought I was the only one dealing with a professional identity crisis. I thought I was crazy for wanting to find a job that would hire me because I brought a variety of work experiences to the table. I thought to myself, who will hire a former art teacher/sometimes practicing artist and quasi graphic designer turned innovation specialist? Where do I fit in? What job am I cut out to do?

I felt ashamed that, despite my degrees and ambition to do great work, I couldn't figure out my career. How could I turn the jungle of my job history into a pretty path that made sense to others? Like many of my peers, I thought it was a myth that I could be everything I wanted to be in my work and be paid for using *all* my identities. How could I find a job that fit me, I wondered, instead of forcing myself to fit a job? I silently suffered until I discovered, and then later opened up about, my hybridity.

Workers with more than one professional identity beat themselves up because no one seems to understand, including themselves, how all their different professional identities fit together. Their overall value is cloudy, so the cycle of despair persists. Even though hybrids enroll in career workshops, purchase tools, and hire coaches to help them make sense of their multiple identities, they don't feel they're making progress. This is because most of the current approaches have a single focus instead of a hybrid orientation.

If you're unsure of your professional identity and how to frame what you do, then it's time to shift your thinking. There are practices to help you do this. The rest of this chapter calls out sources of pain and three things to work on. Once you move through the pain, you'll be ready to embrace your favorite professional identities and see how they support your hybrid professional identity.

Sources of Professional Identity Pain

Returning to Shawn's story, her deep frustration with her professional identity wasn't something that appeared overnight. It was years in the making, and Shawn didn't know what to do about it. Many professionals experience what Shawn went through.

The biggest pain point is that society is missing the right terminology. Few people have heard the term *hybrid professional,* so most don't know that the concept exists. We need the term *hybrid* to more accurately describe employees who have hybrid skills, talents, and identities. Then we can translate how these workers fit into different companies and roles.

Another source of pain is that many hybrid professionals don't *realize* they're hybrids, nor do they realize they're *allowed* to be hybrids. This lack of awareness leads them to continue thinking of themselves in binaries and labeling themselves as either experts or generalists. The fact is they can be both.

The term *expert-generalist* was coined in 2015 by Orit Gadiesh, chairman of Bain & Company. But that's akin to saying a car is a gas-electric vehicle when it's actually a hybrid vehicle that combines gas and electric power in a unique way. In 2010, IDEO, a legendary design firm, coined the term *T-shaped person,* and shortly thereafter, the terms *pi-shaped* and *comb-shaped* were added to this analogy. The *T-shaped person* is also a reference to an expert-generalist. The vertical line of the T represents depth of expertise in one domain and the horizontal bar represents breadth of knowledge across many domains. Pi and comb shapes have more vertical lines, thus they imply a person has more than one vertical of expertise.

Who wants to be called a T-shaped or comb-shaped person? That's an odd and unfamiliar expression. Would you ever start a conversation with, "Hi, I'm a T-shaped professional"? If products can be hybrids, professionals can be, too. The expert-generalist and the T-shaped descriptors don't get to the heart of the matter in quite the same way the word *hybrid* does.

Adam Vicarel described his struggle with being an expert-generalist this way:

> I've battled a bit over the years with deciding whether I should be a jack-of-all-trades and offer a diverse array of services to my

clients, or if I should focus on something more specialized. It's a tough decision, honestly . . . though, I've learned that a jack-of-all-trades and a specialist can be the same thing, depending on how you look at it. You can either see me as "a letter guy," or as a "designer, artist, actor, video maker, photographer, influencer, workshop teacher, speaker," or, as I see myself: I offer all of those diverse things through the filter of "letter guy."

Adam hit the nail on the head. As a hybrid professional, you can be both an expert and a generalist. You can be a specialist because you combine all of your identities into one special set of abilities, and you can be a jack-of-all-trades because you're capable of doing multiple things. They're just blended into a hybrid identity.

Adam thinks of himself as a "letter guy" and all the other things he does are just part of that. Calling himself "letter guy" is his way of expressing his professional identity, but it doesn't capture his hybridity. That's where Adam still has work to do to help the rest of the world see his hybridity and how his identities fit together.

With this realization that workers can be expert-generalists, the next question is what to do about it? Even when people learn the term *hybrid*, they don't know how to hybridize, which means knowing how to work at the intersections of identities. There's an absence of hybrids as role models in the workforce and few career coaches who know how to support their development. People with unrelated work interests, nonlinear career paths, and multiple areas of expertise know these identities fit together, but they don't know how to convey it.

Lack of permission to express hybridity is another source of pain. Without permission, hybrids force themselves to fit the conventions of expert or generalist. They minimize or hide their identities to leverage those that employers or clients prefer. This trick works until it doesn't. If hybrids neglect their other professional identities for too long, they itch to find another job, one that will let them apply their full hybridity. It's important for hybrids to have permission to be hybrids. In fact, it's what they *must* have to be able to show themselves as a complete package.

Unfortunately, most hybrid professionals don't find work that allows them to be a hybrid. After landing job after job that restricts their freedom, hybrids come to believe it's hopeless. They think they'll never find the right role for them. They think no one will ever understand that the reason they're good at what they do is because they blend a special recipe of professional identities, working at the intersections in ways other professionals can't achieve.

Hybrids secretly craft dream job descriptions. They imagine working with clients or employers who recognize hybridity as a desirable and sought-after commodity. They dream of belonging to teams and organizations that value them for their interdisciplinary, cross-sector knowledge and expertise, since it challenges traditions and spawns more innovative thinking and approaches. Until their dream comes true, hybrids wallow in doubt and dissatisfaction at being stuck in hybrid-restrictive roles.

Overcoming the Pain

Professionals who are demoralized, suffering from identity confusion, or feeling intense anxiety about their careers are usually trying to find a solution. Many attempt a professional identity makeover by job hunting, working with a career coach or a resume builder, reading self-help books, and enrolling in workshops, but often it isn't enough. They can sense there's something missing, and they don't know what it is.

Workers who gravitate to the concept of hybrid professionals are deeply committed to finding work they love, know they have something exceptional to offer the world, and believe there's more out there beyond traditional career advice. They just haven't found it yet. They yearn to find the missing lesson that will unlock their professional identity crisis.

What's missing in the career landscape is the existence of hybrid professionals. If you're a professional who's an expert-generalist because you possess skills and knowledge across various disciplines, sectors, industries, and topics, then what should you do about it?

First and foremost: realize you're not alone. I repeat. *You are not alone.* This is a phenomenon that many professionals are experiencing. They feel trapped by titles that box them in, jobs that constrict them to being one kind of professional, and projects that allow them to use only a slim set of their talents.

Hybrid professionals exist. If you think you are one, allow yourself to integrate your professional identities. Then, embrace your hybridity, define it, communicate it, and market your value clearly to the world. When you learn how to do this and can express your hybridity to others, you'll find work that values your full professional self. Like anything worthwhile, this is a process that takes time and self-reflection, but there are steps to help.

Focus on Professional Identities That Light You Up

Going back to my conversation with Shawn, she told me, "I have two degrees, one in finance and one in the liberal arts. I can manage accounts, organize internal processes, set up business systems, and lead teams. I've worked at three large companies, and I've led transitions. Recently, I've been doing consulting. I'm good at many things. I can jump in and provide all types of support, but that's my problem. I'm able to wear too many hats. I'm the jill-of-all-trades, and being a master of none is why no one gets me. How do I communicate what I do?"

I listened to Shawn defend her track record and recount all the things going wrong in her work. I had a good sense of the reasons her professional life was rocky, but I didn't know what she enjoyed doing. Shawn only shared the negative aspects of her work and career, but that wasn't going to move her forward.

To uncover Shawn's hybridity, she needed to identify the professional identities that energized and excited her. Hybridity is formed at the intersections of professional identities that light you up and bring you joy, not the ones that bring you down and you don't want to do. Unless Shawn focused on her favorite professional identities, we'd only be discussing the ones that didn't make her a hybrid.

I asked Shawn to describe moments when she felt the most content and inspired at work. Was she aware of these moments? This was a turning point in the conversation. Shawn told me how she enjoyed facilitating specific workflows, designing better management processes, helping teammates prep for tricky clients, and organizing complex communications. This provided clues to her hybridity, because when Shawn felt her best, it signaled when she was working at the intersections of her primary professional identities. It's not simple to decipher hybridity, but feelings provide clues.

Investigating the intersections of identities requires a lot of reflection. It's also an invitation to think deeply about what you really do for work and why you like certain work-related activities. Brainstorming a list of actions that bring you joy in your job is a great starting point, and it leads to discoveries about how and when identities intersect.

Shift Away from Being a Master of None

Hybrid professionals struggle with feeling as though they're not an expert in anything. Experts are people with deep knowledge and skills in *one* area. Since hybrids are talented in multiple areas, how could they be an expert in many? This contradicts the definition, right? While that statement makes sense, it's not necessarily true for hybrids.

Hybrids are experts in their hybridity. This means that when hybrids mix their multiple identities, they form an altogether new combination of abilities. The sum of their identities is their expertise. Hybrids' expertise lies at the intersections of their identities.

The dilemma is that it's difficult to explain or name this hybrid expertise. There are no universal labels because it's unique—no one else has it. That's also why hybrids get to come up with a name for their own hybrid professional identity.

Here are some questions to ask yourself to unpack your hybrid expertise:

- **What are you best (or in the top twenty-five) at?** It could be on your team, in a company, in a geographic region, or in an industry.
- **What are you the only at?** Onlyness means no one else does what you do.
- **What happens when you integrate your multiple professional identities?** Integration is the distinguishing factor behind hybridity.
- **Who are you at the intersections of your professional identities?** The intersections are where your hybridity is formed. What will you call your hybrid professional identity?

Few people ask themselves these questions, especially the one about what happens when you integrate your multiple professional identities—that one's a doozy. We'll cover the intersections in chapter seven because it's a tough question to answer, and few people are able to generate an answer on the spot.

If you're a hybrid professional, you are a master of something. If you don't know what that is, don't worry because this book will support your discovery. Hybrids have various depths of knowledge in many areas. It's time to stop telling yourself you're a master of none. When you bring all your professional talents together, you are a master of whatever your hybrid professional identity is. That's your value in the world.

Find Roles That Fit You, Not the Other Way Around

One day over lunch, I spoke with Julie Markham, a hybrid professional and Chief Operating Officer for Unreasonable Group, a social impact accelerator. I've known Julie for a few years and have watched her career grow and shift in a short amount of time. Her hybrid journey consists of getting her MBA and master's degree in real estate and construction management, getting into a Techstars Accelerator to launch a startup around safe travel, receiving a Fulbright scholarship, and joining Unreasonable Group to lead global social impact projects.

Julie told me she wanted to work at X, the innovation arm of Google. She had already reached out to a recruiter to gain intel on what it would take to get a job there. Knowing how competitive it was to get hired, Julie wasted no time, and asked the recruiter to examine her resume. She wanted to know the exact language and job titles that the recruiter thought would be the strongest fit, thus upping her chances of getting into the company.

Julie told me the recruiter paused and thought about the question.

"She wasn't sure," Julie recalled, "She saw that I had all kinds of skills, but it wasn't clear what I do. She told me I might be a level 3 or a level 6, Google's terminology for where I fell in their internal management structure. The best she could muster was maybe I fit into business development and should look for opportunities there."

The recruiter's reaction showed how Julie's background, although filled with major accomplishments, was difficult for the recruiter to digest. And the recruiter's suggestion that Julie target business development if she applied wasn't bad advice, but was it the right fit?

Julie is what people call a multitalented professional. She has such a range of talents and accomplishments that it's hard to make sense of her on paper. Her bio is impressive, but also confusing. Even during a screening call, it's challenging to decipher who Julie is as a professional. This is typical for hybrids. The question Julie had to resolve was whether she should be what Google wanted her to be, meaning minimizing her hybridity to get inside? That's the type of thinking many hybrids go through. Julie has to gamble on how to present herself so she looks like the right fit.

This cat-and-mouse game is exhausting for the employer and the job seeker. Hybrid professionals shouldn't have to choose which identities to show or hide. They should show their full hybridity.

Likewise, employers should inquire about hybridity from the start, making it a desirable trait in applicants. Julie had to decide how to pare herself down for the business development position, knowing it wasn't going to fit her hybrid disposition. While there are assumptions here as to what a business development role at Google really entails, the premise is that hybrids need to find hybrid-friendly jobs.

If an employer hires a hybrid professional for one role, and the hybrid decides to be that role, they likely won't be satisfied in the long run. When hybrids suppress one or more of their core identities for a job, they sacrifice part of how they operate, think, and perform. That job is not the right fit.

The only way for hybrid professionals to find work they love is to make their hybridity explicit to employers, clients, and colleagues. When hybrids are job searching, they should leverage their hybridity as an asset from the outset. That way, the full suite of their professional identities is known, and more importantly, people see how those different identities relate to one another and why that matters to their role.

The relationships between identities is what matters most in hybridity. Articulating how these identities connect is what makes someone a hybrid, and why they provide unique value. Defining hybridity helps employers, clients, and colleagues understand why a hybrid is the right fit. Hybrids need work that leverages their hybridity, not work that forces them to choose between professional identities and minimizes their full value.

It's time to move beyond the pain of nobody knowing what you do. Realize you can be a hybrid professional. Learning how to express your varied expertise is what makes you a hybrid, and it will help you find work that allows you to be your full professional self.

KEY IDEAS ABOUT HYBRID PROFESSIONALS

- Know you're not alone. Others struggle to be seen for their multiple identities, too. Realize the term *hybrid professionals* exists and start using it.

- Be clear on the professional identities that are your strengths and the ones you love. Stop focusing on those you *don't* want to be known for. Broadcast your favorite identities so they shine. Diminish the ones you want to let go.

- Shift away from thinking you're a jack-of-all-trades but master of none. You can be good at a lot of things and be a master of many identities. That's hybridity in action.

- Don't force yourself into roles that aren't designed for you or your hybridity. If you sacrifice parts of your professional identity to get a job, you'll never find a role that celebrates your full hybridity.

CHAPTER 2

Are You a Hybrid Professional?

"Having more diversified knowledge and being a jack-of-all-trades actually allows you to master knowledge that is farther away from your expertise in ways that can be beneficial. That can have important impacts on the future of science, the future of ideas, and innovation for companies."

—**Frank Nagle, assistant professor, Strategy Unit,
Harvard Business School**

BEFORE REALIZING THAT I was a hybrid professional, I found a lot of words that I thought described me: multidimensional, polymath, Renaissance soul, multipotentialite, multihyphenate, boundary crosser, slash, cross-pollinator, connector, nonconformist, T-shaped, multipassionate, multitalented, pluralist, and job crafter.

But none of these terms truly fit me because they're synonyms for having more than one identity or doing many things for work. That wasn't what I was. I wasn't a collector of multiple identities. I was an integrator who fused identities together. What word conveyed that? It took me awhile to find it, just as others are seeking it too.

"I have many lives," Bono said in an interview, alluding to his professional identities as a musician, venture capitalist, philanthropist, businessman, and social activist. As the lead singer of the band U2, even Bono is not immune from the struggles of multidimensionality. He's constantly navigating how his fans see him, how the world sees him, and how he sees himself.

At one point, Bono was named "the face of fusion philanthropy" because he brings together religious leaders, politicians, government officials, humanitarian organizations, media outlets, and relief workers to advance social missions on international issues around violence, hunger, world peace, and AIDS. Calling Bono a *fusion philanthropist* is merely a synonym for saying he's a hybrid.

Bono's hybridity appears in everything he does, whether it's philanthropic or musical. U2's songs are full of calls for social injustices, which sometimes causes controversy and criticism. Why does U2 create music about civil rights protests and wars when they can sing about anything? Some people may question why U2 blends politics with music, but that's what happens when professionals have multiple identities. Genres, values, ideas, and beliefs collide. Tensions appear at the intersections and have to be negotiated.

Bono acknowledges that he feels torn about how best to blend his professional identities. In a 2014 article in *The Guardian*, he explained:

> I thought I could use this absurdity, celebrity, and I managed to turn it into currency and go to work with it, but then at some point it became difficult to be in a band and bring your baggage to this issue. So I've tried to keep my head down and wait for the right moment to put it up.

Being a hybrid professional and being accepted for the way you combine your identities are tricky. Bono's a superstar, and his decisions and actions are in the public eye. He knows he can use that status for good, but he also realizes that there's a time and a place to weave together his identities.

Likewise, Gail Simmons, famous for being a judge on the Food Network's *Top Chef* series and for leading special projects for *Food & Wine* magazine, didn't realize she could weave her professional identities together. As she explained in a podcast:

> When I started out in the food world, I really didn't understand that it could be a job. . . . It really took someone else objectively pointing that out to me. These are the things you love—you love to travel, you love to write, you love food, eating, and cooking, and sharing that experience with people. Why can't you make that a job? And, it literally dumbfounded me because I hadn't thought of it that way before. I was so worried about finding a

professional track and fitting into careers that were already very obviously laid out before me. Creating something of my own, creating something new, didn't come naturally. I don't think I was a natural entrepreneur, but once it was shown to me in that light, I could move forward in that direction.

One reason for Simmons's success is her hybridity. Instead of fitting into existing roles, she connected her professional interests, expertise, and identities to differentiate herself from others. This helped her carve her own path in the food and entertainment industry. Leading special projects for *Food & Wine* is a nice way of saying Simmons is a hybrid, and they don't know what title to give her.

The notion that workers can only be experts or generalists is outdated. Today there are three types of professional identity: *singularity, multiplicity,* and *hybridity* (Figure 1). People with one professional identity fall into the category of singularity. These are typically experts or specialists. People with two or more professional identities fall into the category of multiplicity. These are typically generalists, multitalented professionals, freelancers, and so forth. But people who have two or more professional identities that intersect, like in a Venn diagram, fall into the category of hybridity. I'll talk more about these three identity types in Chapter 5.

Figure 1. *Three Types of Professional Identity*

What Is a Hybrid?

A hybrid is a fusion. Hybrid cars combine gas and electric power. Hybrid foods like the sushiritto combine sushi and burritos. Hybrid medications like Theraflu target multiple symptoms. Hybrid utensils like sporks combine a spoon and a fork. And hybrid products like toothpaste fight cavities and whiten teeth at the same time.

Hybridity is a fascinating concept because there are so many types: biological, ethnic, linguistic, and cultural, just to name a few. Biological hybridity involves the cross-fertilization of plants into new species. Ethnic hybridity describes people who are biracial or binational. Basically, when a mixture of elements occurs, hybridity is present.

Hybrids are all around us. They're formed all the time as a result of solving a need, happy accidents, or intentional mixing. After a while, hybrids don't seem new because they become an ordinary part of life. It's hard to remember existing without them, but at one point, there was no name for a given odd combination of things until someone invented it, it was adopted by many, and then it stuck. Importantly, the examples I listed of different kinds of hybrids all show a key characteristic of hybridity: their multiple properties are fully integrated.

For instance, if I had a backpack with multiple objects in it, and I called it a hybrid backpack, that wouldn't make sense because those objects have nothing to do with the backpack or how it functions. They're all independent objects that happen to be inside the backpack. Whereas if the backpack was in the form of a bladder with a straw in it to make it a new version of a wearable water bottle, well, that's a hybrid backpack. Instead of calling it a water bottle/backpack, a company called CamelBak designs them as their product line.

We live and interact with a sea of hybrid products. New ideas come onto the market by combining existing features and functions. Sometimes we see hybridity, and other times we're oblivious to it. Hybridity produces things that have yet to be named, and combinations of things that have never existed before—this applies to the world of work, too.

What Is a Hybrid Professional?

Hybrid professionals have existed for centuries. The Renaissance man of the 1400s evolved into the polymath and the triple threat of the 1900s, and now the job crafter and slashie of the 2000s. If we look back, there are scores of historical figures who fit these terms, from Aristotle and Leonardo

DaVinci to Marie Curie, Helen Keller, and Fred Astaire. They embody being a hybrid professional.

Hybrid professionals are everywhere. Hybrids can be famous, and hybrids can be in regular nine-to-five jobs. You encounter them at the grocery store, in other countries, and in the media. They're often disguised as experts or generalists in offices, on teams, or working on their own. You don't know if someone is a hybrid professional until you learn about their professional identity.

People ask me if anyone can be a hybrid professional, and the answer is yes. People ask me if all professionals are hybrid professionals, and the answer is no. It's no because like any identity construct, if someone perceives themselves to have a certain identity, then they *are* that identity. We create our professional identities. If someone believes they are a hybrid professional, then they are. But, not everyone is a hybrid.

My definition of a hybrid professional is a person who integrates multiple professional identities and works from the intersections of those identities. Hybrid professionals *integrate* rather than *separate* multiple identities. Their value lies in the unique relationships of those identities. The two fundamental concepts behind hybrid professional identity are integration and interrelationships of identities.

Professional identity is the identity or identities a person uses in their work, whether or not they get paid for it. Work isn't necessarily about employment or how someone makes a living. For instance, a board member, a stay-at-home parent, a volunteer, or an intern may all consider those activities to be their work. All fall under the umbrella of their professional identity.

Much of professional identity is self-defined. If someone changes careers or roles in a company and believes they still possess their old professional identity, then it's up to them whether they want to carry it forward and maintain that identity alongside their new identity. That's why it's important not to assume that a person's job title defines them.

Hybrid professionals lead and create novel experiences, products, and services because they combine talents and skills in unforeseen ways. In the intersections of their different identities, hybrids form new connections and new ways of working. This is where a hybrid's unique value lies.

Hybrid professionals must learn how to name and define their intersections. This can be hard to do because those intersections encapsulate elements from each of the conjoined parts. For me, this means I have to describe how my artist, educator, designer, and researcher identities fit together. If I introduce myself only as these four identities, I sound like a list of different identities as opposed to sounding like a synthesis of all of them. I call myself a *creative disruptor* because I feel that represents what happens when I merge my four identities together. You can see how someone else would name their intersection something different, even if they have similar primary professional identities to mine, because their hybridity is different than mine.

Complicating the naming and defining of the intersections is the fact that intersections are unconscious spaces of working. Few professionals realize when they're working in them. You can learn how to pay attention to and heighten your awareness of these intersections (you'll more on this in Chapters 7 and 8.) Knowing how you cross identities and what happens when you do is what distinguishes you as a hybrid.

What Scholars Say About Hybrid Identity

Homi Bhabha, a scholar and critical theorist, has developed several significant concepts, including the term *cultural hybridity.* He writes extensively about hybridization and post-colonialism to examine power dynamics between colonizers and the colonized. He looks at these spaces of tension to study cultural hybridity and its impact on contemporary society.

I mention Bhabha's work because his ideas about cultural hybridity also apply to hybrid professional identity. In his book *The Location of Culture,* he writes about a space:

in-between the designations of identity . . . this interstitial passage between fixed identifications opens up the possibility of a cultural hybridity that entertains difference without an assumed or imposed hierarchy.

Bhabha's reference of the interstitial space between fixed identities describes that new potential exists that doesn't conform to the rules or hierarchies of either identity. This is an emboldened space that allows differences to collide. This is one way of thinking about the power of hybrid identity.

Another way to think about hybrid identity is in a passage from Mikhail Bakhtin, a literary theorist and critic who studied intertextuality in language:

> The . . . hybrid is not only double-voiced and double-accented . . . but is also double-languaged; for in it there are not only (and not even so much) two individual consciousnesses, two voices, two accents, as there are [doublings of] socio-linguistic conscious-nesses, two epochs . . . that come together and consciously fight it out . . . It is the collision between differing points of view on the world that are embedded in these forms . . . such unconscious hybrids have been at the same time profoundly productive histor-ically; they are pregnant with potential for new world views, with new 'internal forms' for perceiving the world in words.

The phrases "collision between differing points of view" and "pregnant with potential" are profound sentiments about the interstitial spaces. While these are theoretical lenses, they shed light on hybridity. Hybrid identity is about doubleness. When two identities unite, they bring their own attributes independent of each other. In the collisions, tension appears and suddenly a new way of seeing the world emerges. Hybrid identity entertains difference through doubleness.

Hybrid identity suggests that multiple, unrelated identi-ties can coexist, and when combined, they can cocreate new identities. Hybrid identity implies uncharted conceptions of self within the interstitial spaces. These conceptions are ambiguous and boundless, and have no fixed order. Identities can carry different weight and importance at different times.

> "When identities interconnect, they inform and influence one another. This is an entirely new identity—a hybrid identity—the sum of other identities."

The concept of hybrid workers isn't new, but the term hasn't caught on. Journals in the 1990s focused on hybrid managers, and only a handful of online articles in the 2000s mention hybrid professionals. I began studying hybrid professional identity around 2012. I set a Google alert for the term "hybrid professionals" to observe the latest information being published.

Week after week, as the top results appeared in my inbox, I was dismayed. Instead of receiving interesting articles about hybrid jobs or the career successes of hybrid professionals, the alert filled my inbox with headlines that read like this:

"Wind Solar Hybrid Systems Market Summary"

"Global Automotive Hybrid Transmissions in Demand"

"Hybrid Operating Room Gaining Traction in Urban Healthcare"

Where were the stories, research articles, and popular headlines about hybrid professionals, not just hybrid products and technologies, I wondered. After a while, I stopped reading the alerts. When I randomly peeked, they continued to trend toward hybrid technologies, discoveries, and environmental issues.

This confirmed two things. First, hybridity is a popular term within science, technology, and environmental studies, but it's absent in studies of people and professional identity. Second, even though hybrid professionals are on the rise, hybrid professional identity hasn't entered academic literature or the mainstream.

Clues for Spotting a Hybrid

From the late 1980s into the 1990s, Isaac Mizrahi was a major force in the fashion industry in New York City. I had always thought of him as a fashion designer, until I heard his TED Talk, in which he said:

> I don't really think of myself as a designer, and I don't really think of myself necessarily as a fashion designer, and frankly I don't really know what to call myself. I think of myself as um . . . oh, I don't know what I think of myself as. So, that's just that . . . I love to cook. And I often look at things as though they're food. Like I say, oh, you know, would you serve a rotten chicken, then how could you serve, you know, a beat-up old dress or something? I always relate things to kitchenry.

In describing food, Mizrahi references clothing, an uncommon comparison and one that shows his way of seeing the world. It's a clue to his hybridity. His range of professional identities is wide and has been noted by the media. He does cabaret, hosts TV shows, writes books, appears in movies, is a celebrity judge, and still designs fashion collections. The editor of *Cosmopolitan* commented on his evolution from fashion designer to "polymath — businessman, entertainer."

A 2013 *New York Times* article stated that Mizrahi is "distracted by his interests in set design, acting and hosting talk and reality shows, he's been too unfocused to develop a signature style that might once have propelled him into the pantheon of great American designers." While that's a harsh critique, the plight of a hybrid professional is that their array of professional identities can make them seem unfocused. Even though hybrids may appear scattered, they usually haven't found how to convey their hybridity. That's why their professional pursuits sound fragmented instead of integrated.

Lexie Smith describes herself as a "multiperson" on her LinkedIn header, but based on the nature of what she does and how she does it, she meets the criteria of being a hybrid professional. Smith is said to be "one to skirt labels," an idea that's emphasized in the name of her personal website, allsemantics.com. Perhaps it's her way of illustrating a refusal to be typecast.

Smith declines to be called a pastry chef, although that's the position she's held at cafés and restaurants in Manhattan.

On her website, she refers to herself as a baker and multimedia artist. Growing up, she was fascinated by making things, but says she never would have called herself an artist. Early in life, she was obsessed with writing, sewing, bookbinding, and poetry, and she started baking when she was in high school.

Smith rose to fame for her fashion sense, being featured in posts in *Vogue,* and later became known for her creations of sculptural loaves of bread. She applies artistry to bread baking, turning challah into an arching serpent, or stretching dough into symbolic shapes rooted in religious or cultural ideologies. Her unexpected creations are works of art, edible sculptures, and social commentaries.

For an interview in *Vice News,* Smith said, "If you look at bread, you have to look at subsidies and revolts and taxation. Bread has never really been simple." She launched the website Bread on Earth, where she explores the potential of bread as a metaphor and a physical substance. She seeks to engage people in dialogue around social and political issues where bread is a starting point, since it's a common staple across civilizations.

Between using bread as a medium for change and fusing culinary, cultural, and artistic worlds, Smith is a model of hybridity. Journalists say she "is no stranger to the creative realm and to the act of pushing her own creative boundaries far beyond comfort," and she is the only bread artist leading conversations about bread politics, both signs she's a hybrid.

Reflecting on Mizrahi and Smith, here are five attributes common to hybrids:

Hybrids love trying out new combinations. Smith creates sculptures from bread and Mizrahi talks about fashion as food. Hybrids enjoy mixing, tinkering, and hacking. They naturally work across disciplines to make things others never dreamed of. Non-hybrids like to create, but they're less inclined to radically mix things together the way hybrids do.

Hybrids possess rarity or onlyness. Smith is the only artist/bread baker exploring bread's potential as a social barometer through Bread on Earth. Mizrahi never wanted to create a signature look, but his fashions have a distinctive sense of color and humor that tell you he made it. Hybrids do things that only they, or very few, can do. They have rare gifts and talents. They make magic happen and deliver more than what others think is possible.

Words fail to describe hybrids. It's hard to describe Smith's bread sculptures or Mizrahi's designs without seeing them, and it's hard to give either of them a job title. They can't be put into a box. A hybrid's work has to be seen or interacted with to be understood, like describing the taste of a bizarre ice cream flavor, the sound of a new musical composition, or the choreography of a dance.

Hybrids have their own process and style of doing things. How does Smith turn bread into art? She probably uses artistic and baking techniques in her own special way. Hybrids use original methods to achieve their results.

They connect dots across domains to break conventions and make up their own style. Non-hybrids stick to tried-and-true processes that are hardly surprising to follow.

Hybrids see connections and patterns where others don't. Mizrahi sees kitchenry and thinks of fashion. It may sound bizarre, but it's how he thinks. Smith sees bread as a connector of social, political, economic, and ecological forces. Hybrids might bring together collaborators from different subject areas because they see relatedness and possibilities. Non-hybrids see this as overcomplicating or making projects bigger than necessary.

Aside from these clues, hybrids generally meet four criteria:
- They possess multiple professional identities.
- They have a clear set of primary professional identities.
- They effortlessly integrate primary professional identities.
- They find flow and enjoyment at the intersections of their primary professional identities.

These criteria needn't be inherent—there are ways to evolve into hybridity. Some of them are developmental, some are learned, and some have to do with gaining more work experience. Learning how to cross and combine professional identities into a hybrid identity takes patience, persistence, and the accumulation of diverse experiences.

Part Two explains the developmental construct behind hybrid professional identity. Some people may be *emerging hybrids,* while others are *fully developed hybrids.* As hybrids advance in their careers and acquire additional identities, their hybridity may become stronger and more pronounced. They stumble into and out of their intersections—the emerging stage—until they settle in and own their hybridity. Without guidance to support their development, emerging hybrids may flounder to grasp their hybridity. It's not necessarily obvious to perceive hybridity without help. To be fully developed, hybrids must learn to convey their uniqueness to others and know that their intersections are what make them rare at what they do for work.

Are Job Changers Automatically Hybrid Professionals?

It depends. People who get knocked for being job hoppers or unfocused career dabblers may or may not be hybrids. The number of people who stay at one company or in one career is diminishing and workers are gaining more skills and credentials along the way. The workforce is rapidly changing. Our concept of what a career is and who professionals are is not keeping pace.

In 2019, Rafael Sarandeses, who calls himself a career fitness professor, wrote:

> We are living through the transformation of manufacturing through automation and the related decline in middle-class employment in which hours of work are traded for wages and security . . . it is possible that the progressive application of technology and artificial intelligence to different professional lines of

work will have unprecedented effects in the configuration of the labor market as we currently know it.

A 2017 study by McKinsey estimated that by the year 2030, about 14 percent of the global workforce, roughly 375 million workers, may be forced to learn new skills or undergo career transitions. This is due to automation, digital disruption, and artificial intelligence.

People hold an average of 11.7 jobs between the ages of eighteen and forty-eight. This statistic was reported in March 2015 by the US Bureau of Labor Statistics, which conducted a longitudinal study of people born between 1957 to 1964. For this study, they defined a job as an uninterrupted period of work with an employer.

Researcher Bettina Lankard Brown studies professionals who make major swerves in their career trajectories, particularly those who start over to follow new interests. Brown notes that "the linear career path that once kept people working in the same job is not the standard career route for today's workers. Instead, many workers are now pursuing varied career paths that reflect sequential career changes."

Brown shared two examples:

- Alan Goldstein, who, in response to his growing interest in computer technology, resigned from his career as a trauma surgeon at Kings County Hospital in New York, and, at age forty-nine, formed his own software company

- Glenn Gainley, who, after working his way up to vice president in charge of business units at Symbios, Inc., quit his job at age forty and returned to school to pursue a teaching career

Career paths are becoming unbounded, as evidenced by the emergence of the gig economy, which is defined as workers who earn income outside of traditional, long-term employment. According to a 2019 post by the Gig Economy Data Hub, a joint effort of the Aspen Institute's Future of Work Initiative and Cornell University's ILR School, more than a quarter of American workers take part in the gig economy in some capacity, and more than one in ten workers rely on gig work for their primary income. It's estimated that 55 million people are actively engaged in the gig economy, making it the largest growing area of the nation's workforce.

These job statistics illustrate that a substantial number of people hold nontraditional jobs to earn income, and people change jobs every two and a half years. Workers who fit these statistics tend to have more than one professional identity. Not all of them are hybrid professionals, but many may be. Hybrids are spread throughout the working population. Until further studies are conducted, it's hard to know how many hybrids are in the workforce since many workers are undergoing different job transitions.

The takeaway here is that professionals who seem scattered or drift in their career pursuits may be either trying to find a career they love or they may be hybrids searching for acceptance for their full hybridity. When workers accumulate identities and realize those identities form interconnected relationships, that's when hybridity takes root.

How I Became a Hybrid Professional

I am more than my job title. I always have been, but I didn't always know that about myself. Today, I am the epitome of a hybrid professional, and I'm a researcher of hybrid professionals because I'm so passionate about this concept. I have a full-time job as the director of a wonderful initiative focused on connecting and catalyzing stakeholders around challenges in child development. This role allows me to use my hybridity, and I draw upon my artist, educator, designer, and researcher identities every day. Getting hired for this role demonstrated to me that hybrid jobs do exist, and that it's possible to find work that truly suits my hybridity.

However, before my current job, I went through a long period where I felt stuck in my career. I empathize with anyone who doesn't feel seen or valued for their multiple identities. I felt that way until I discovered my hybridity.

I was tired of employers, coworkers, and colleagues thinking of me as only an art teacher, since that's how I made my living for a number of years. I saw myself as more than a teacher, but I didn't know how to show that my other identities as an artist, designer, and innovator were important parts of who I was at that time. I thought I had to choose between my various identities and could only get paid for being one at a time. I also lacked clarity in how to convey this to others.

Ten years ago, I was teaching in a classroom setting. Since then, I've gone from being an art program coordinator to an art teacher to leading innovation efforts in K–12 schools to building entrepreneurial ecosystems across communities. I never envisioned my career taking this trajectory. The last three job titles I've held are positions that didn't exist when I was in college. I've followed a nonlinear career path, which has helped me form my hybridity because I expanded my experiences and crossed a wide range of disciplines.

It took a professional identity crisis, a series of job changes, exposure to cultural theories, and lots of self-reflection to realize I'm a hybrid. Before that revelation, I carried intense shame and guilt that I didn't know what my professional identity was, and it seemed that everyone else knew theirs. I dreaded being asked what I did because it felt insincere to introduce myself as a teacher. I wanted to break free from that label. I was conscious of the weight titles hold both outwardly and inwardly as a measure of who we are.

The realization that I'm a hybrid professional happened in stages. First, I quit my job as a teacher because I didn't think I was achieving my potential. I could tell something was missing, and I wasn't using all of my talents or identities. The sensation of feeling incomplete or constricted is common for hybrids. It's a sign that we're not using all of our multiple identities.

About this time, I stumbled across the book *Teaching 2030* by Barnett Berry. In it, he used the term *teacherpreneurs* to describe teachers who lead but don't leave the classroom. This concept fascinated me. I loved the combination of *teacher* and *entrepreneur* as a new word. And, I was enchanted with the idea of being both a teacher and a leader in the community. That sounded like my dream job. It was also a hybrid job. The problem was no one was hiring for it because the concept was more theoretical than practical, but it left a mark on me.

So, I enrolled in a doctoral program and got a part-time job that didn't involve teaching, but did involve creativity and entrepreneurship. I didn't see it at the time, but that was a hybrid job. To land this job, I tried something different. For the application, I explicitly listed my professional identities in my cover letter to show I was more than a teacher.

In the opening paragraph, I stated, "I'm Sarabeth Berk, and I consider myself to be an artist/teacher/designer and that matters to this role because…" and then I explained how each identity supported that position. This strategy proved effective because it helped my employer see the exact identities I felt I was bringing, and I showed my value across multiple domains. To this day, I use this technique when applying for jobs, and I've found it to be useful. The trick is to list only your primary professional identities, those you really want to be known for, and clearly show how they're related to the role you want.

During my doctoral studies, I did a lot of self-reflection. Professors asked us to write numerous papers about our values, our beliefs, and our identity, and then support it with academic literature. This exposed me to theories that have become pivotal to my understanding and analysis of hybrids. In particular, I was influenced by intersectionality by Kimberlé Crenshaw, a/r/tography by Rita Irwin and Stephanie Springgay, heterotopias by Michael Foucault, and third space by Homi Bhabha. The final ingredient that impacted me was the devices Surrealists use to create their artworks.

The result of this period of deep reflection was that I realized I had multiple professional identities and that I was allowed to have them, and other people were too. I saw that although we use the generic job titles of teacher, professor, marketer, salesperson, and designer, we are more than our job titles. Job titles are narrow definitions of who we are.

Learning about intersectionality and third space was the tipping point for me. Those theories caused me to ask the question that if people have more than one professional identity, and those identities intersect, could they work from the spaces between their professional identities? That became my research question.

The answer was yes. In the intersections is where hybrid professional identity exists. And, a whole new type of professional is born. That was when I had the epiphany that I was a hybrid professional.

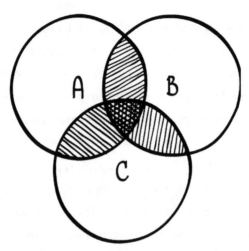

Figure 2. Venn diagrams can help you investigate the intersections in your identities.

I started drawing Venn diagrams, mapping my identities in each circle, and investigating the intersections (Figure 2). It was the beginning of my professional identity awakening. After I figured out the concept of hybrid professional identity, and realized it applied to me, my career trajectory didn't immediately become hybrid. It took a few years post-graduation and a couple of jobs to learn how to put this into practice. Partially, this is because I didn't know how to apply the concept to my own experience yet. Also, I didn't have the right tools to talk about hybridity so people understood what I meant and why it mattered to the workforce. Over time, I tested and refined my thinking.

Today, I'm proud to call myself a hybrid professional. My primary identities include artist, educator, research, and designer—these are critical to how I work every day and are inextricably linked to shaping my expertise. *Creative disruptor* is the hybrid job title I created to define myself and how I want to be known; I use my various identities to transform systems and develop creative solutions that bring people together to collaborate in new and impactful ways.

Realizing that I don't have to compartmentalize who I am and that my professional identities can exist together in harmony has brought me contentment and empowered me in my career. I don't hide the fact that I possess four professional identities, and I don't try to fit into one box anymore or pick roles that don't allow all of my identities to shine. Owning my hybridity has changed my life and the trajectory of my career.

Has it made finding a job easier now that I know my hybridity? No, I think finding a job that's the right fit will always be a process. It has helped me get stronger and be clearer about my professional brand, what I stand for, what I'm really good at, and what sets me apart from every other person who does innovation work like I do. I feel more confident that I know how to articulate my professional value and I believe that helps me attract and seek opportunities that are a good match for me.

Are you a hybrid professional? After almost a decade of studying professional identity among a variety of professionals, I can say I underestimated the size of the problem I set out to solve for myself. Today, physical therapists, financial advisors, executive assistants, freelancers, teachers, college students, computer coders, marketers, designers, musicians, librarians, coaches, and many other professionals have reached out to me because this topic resonates with them.

Professionals from all fields are more than their titles. Like me, they possess multiple professional identities and integrate their professional identities together to become hybrid professionals. They struggle to be understood for how their different professional identities fit together, and they struggle to convey the value of their hybridity to employers and clients. They think they're alone in this phenomenon, yet they're not.

KEY IDEAS ABOUT HYBRID PROFESSIONALS

- Test whether you might be a hybrid professional by asking yourself, "What are my professional identities?" If you know your professional identities, then try answering: "Who am I, or what am I doing, when I integrate my multiple identities?" If you get stumped, don't worry, most people do. The intersections are hard to describe. Part Two dives deeper into the intersections.

- Notice the professional identities you've accumulated from your work experiences. Hybridity evolves as you gain more identities. Pay attention to your core or primary professional identities. Hybridity is formed from those.

- Revisit the list of five clues about hybrid professionals, and think about how these may or may not apply to you:

    - Hybrids love trying out new combinations.
    - Hybrids possess rarity or onlyness.
    - Words fail to describe hybrids.
    - Hybrids have their own process and style of doing things.
    - Hybrids see connections and patterns where others don't.

CHAPTER 3

How Do You Answer
What Do You Do?

"My kids ask me what I do, and I don't have a good answer
for them. There is something pejorative about all labels."
—Alex Bogusky, co-founder and chief creative engineer,
Crispin Porter Bogusky

ONE NIGHT DURING STARTUP Week, an event that brings the entrepreneur community together, my friend tugged on my wrist and exclaimed, "You have to come see this!"

We dashed out into the street where a shiny Airstream trailer with the words "Crave Design Factory" painted on its sides was parked on the corner. Both the door and the window flaps were propped open, and an electric glow emanated from the interior. I could tell we were about to experience something strange and unforgettable.

A sign on the door read, "Build-a-Vibe Workshop," with an arrow pointing inside. We crossed the threshold into a modern-looking showroom that was clean, hip, and mysterious. I started examining the beautifully crafted products displayed on short white shelves, trying to make sense of the unusual shapes and sizes. Another neon sign hung above the shelves that read, "Own Your Pleasure." I realized that not only were the products pleasing to look at, but they were also pleasing to touch. The Airstream trailer was a well-branded, pop-up sex shop.

The co-founder of Crave, and this traveling shop, walked over and greeted my friend and me. She told us her name was Ti Chang. Of course, I asked her, "What do you do?"

Ti was more than the co-founder; she was a master of helping women own their sexual pleasure, an accomplished industrial designer, a brilliant marketer, and a savvy businesswoman. She told us how she started her career as a product designer for a major company, but saw a need to transform the sex toy market and change stigma around women's pleasure. She was now a leader in the emerging space of sextech. The Crave Design Factory was a business strategy to tour the country, market their unique vibrators, and open healthy dialogue around sexual pleasure.

I was hardly ready for what happened next. Ti led me to a small workbench at the side of the showroom and guided me through how to build my own vibe. It was a DIY workshop she invented to create an educational experience and get people comfortable talking about sex toys.

I noticed Ti was wearing a beautiful pendant necklace, and I asked her about it. It turned out it wasn't an ordinary necklace. The pendant was one of their best-selling products, the Vesper Vibrator Necklace. It was a miniature vibrator designed to be worn as a piece of jewelry in public and used for pleasure, instead of hidden away in a drawer that never saw the light of day. The Vesper broke every convention I had about sex toys as being shameful, awkward hunks of plastic. This necklace was sleek, luxurious, and beautiful. I admired it on Ti like any other fashionable item I've seen on a woman's body.

Ti is a hybrid professional. Her company, Crave, is an example of her hybridity in action, and so are her products. Ti is more than her job title of co-founder, and her answer to *what do you do* isn't straightforward. How would you explain what Ti does?

The role of First Lady is one of the most well-known and public positions in American society. It's also one that allows for maximum hybrid professional identity. Not only can a First Lady design the role to be whatever she wants, she can flex in and out of societal issues that she is passionate about and has experience in.

Vogue did a story about Michelle Obama during her tenure as First Lady, and the author of the story, Jonathan Van Meter, noted that the role of First Lady is peculiar:

> She has a job with no salary, a platform with no power, an East Wing filled with staff but no budget. And it is, as Mrs. Obama will

point out to me later, a role that is surprisingly malleable, shaped by the personality, style, and interests (or lack thereof) of the person occupying it.

In that same interview, Mrs. Obama said:

> I could have spent eight years doing anything, and at some level, it would have been fine. I could have focused on flowers. I could have focused on decor. I could have focused on entertainment. Because any First Lady, rightfully, gets to define her role. There's no legislative authority; you're not elected. And that's a wonderful gift of freedom.

The beauty of the title First Lady is that it's not bound to one definition. It's open to being defined. It was in this role that Mrs. Obama's hybrid professional identity came alive, perhaps for the first time in her career.

In a different interview, Mrs. Obama spoke about blending her professional identities and what that looked like as First Lady:

> But there is a method to my madness. There's a reason why I've been out there jumping rope and hula hooping and dancing to Beyoncé, whatever it takes. It's because I want kids to see that there are all kinds of ways to be active. And if I can do it, anybody can do it.

Mrs. Obama is a former lawyer who has held executive positions in nonprofits, including a university and a major medical center. She has been a community leader and an advocate. Jumping rope and hula hooping as First Lady showed how she wove her professional identities into something new.

Let's Move was a program she designed to encourage healthier living. It didn't look or sound anything like her former work experiences because her professional identities merged into something else. The programs and initiatives she worked on during her time in the White House showed her hybridity in action.

Becoming First Lady was a career shift for Mrs. Obama and, without a predefined set of expectations, she molded it into her own vision. Previously, she considered herself to be a rule follower who took a linear approach to her career. "I narrowed myself to being this thing I thought I should be," she said in 2018 when she was asked about her journey. "It took loss—losses in my life that made me think, 'Have you ever stopped to think about who you wanted to be?'"

Today, it's impossible to give Mrs. Obama a job title. How do you think she would answer the question *what do you do?* She has a host of professional identities as an author, speaker, advocate, lawyer, and philanthropist to name a few. Yet, we know her as Mrs. Obama, the compilation of all those identities because she's more than one title.

I started calling myself a hybrid professional a couple years ago. It felt radical and abnormal to label myself this way at first, so I shied away from telling it to people. I was scared they'd think I was weird or would understand me less.

I don't have that fear anymore. The more people I talk to about being a hybrid professional, the more acceptance, support, and connection I find among other professionals. The concept immediately clicks, and usually they want to learn more about me or more about how they might be a hybrid too.

I had no idea that would be the case. After feeling like I was the only one experiencing tension between having multiple professional identities, it has been eye-opening to meet so many workers who are dealing with this same dilemma. Now, when I'm asked what I do, I answer with, "I'm a hybrid professional. I combine my artist/researcher/educator/designer identities together to transform systems and lead innovation strategies. What do you do?"

Alain de Botton is a philosopher and the creator of the School of Life, an educational company that offers life advice. De Botton calls the *what do you do* remark the most iconic question of the twenty-first century. In an interview, he stated:

> Our identities are entirely bound up with our work. You can't really understand someone without understanding what their job is. . . . In other words, there is a real danger of a disconnect between what's on your business card, and who you are deep inside, and it's not a disconnect that the world is ready to be patient with.

This danger of that disconnect is felt by professionals of all kinds, even those who aren't hybrids. Society defines and judges us by how we introduce ourselves. This is why there's so much anxiety, self-confidence, and self-worth wrapped up with professional introductions. We've been conditioned to associate who a person is with what they do, even though we know job titles and professions offer an incomplete picture of a person.

To complicate matters, Malcolm Gladwell writes in his book *Blink* about a phenomenon called *thin-slicing* and how it affects first impressions. Thin-slicing is the act of making snap judgments based on the thinnest of experiences. Even though our judgments happen unconsciously, they impact our view of ourselves and our ability to interact with something or someone.

In those critical first moments, we are processing a lot of information quickly, and that includes a person's introduction of themselves. This is why our answer to the *what do you do* question and our job title are critical, because they happen in that brief window of thin-slicing when people make snap judgments. This is why we feel pressure to nail our answers to the what do you question to make a good first impression and encourage snap judgments in our favor.

Now, imagine the person you're meeting for the first time is a hybrid, and they have multiple professional identities. How do you think they'll answer the *what do you do* question? In their heads, they know they have to quickly make one of three choices based on the situation and their thin-slicing of you. A hybrid can introduce themselves as only one professional identity, introduce themselves by listing as many of their professional identities as they like, or evade the question by making some offhand remark such as "I do a bunch of things." Most hybrids I've met go for the second option and list their professional identities.

As someone who studies hybrid professionals, I can tell you that none of the three options is very effective in conveying who hybrids are. I've created a short and simple script for hybrids to introduce themselves, and I've seen it work well. It's explained later in this chapter.

The most important part of the introduction is to merely say, "Hi, I'm a hybrid professional." That phrase alone, saying you're a hybrid professional, immediately cues your listener and opens the door. They become intrigued and usually want to get to know more about what that means. As de Botton said, the world is not nearly patient enough to get to know the full you beyond your title, so this quick trick extends the timetable so you have more time to reveal who you are.

It's complicated for hybrids to answer the *what do you do* question. Words are arbitrary and mean different things to different people. It will always be hard to convey hybridity through language alone. Take Neri Oxman, for example. Her professional identities span four disciplines, and people don't know how to describe what she does.

In basic terms, Oxman is a prominent contemporary artist and professor at MIT. Her work is in the collection of the Smithsonian, and she has been featured in *Wired* magazine. She appears fearless and unconcerned with how people perceive her. She knows she's doing innovative work that people struggle to comprehend.

One time, her staff ordered 6,500 silkworms for Silk Pavilion, a three-meter-diameter dome that was constructed using silkworms in combination with a robotic arm that was also spinning silk. Together the silkworms and robot demonstrated alternative methods of manufacturing, essentially creating a living material design structure. Obviously, the purchasing department at MIT, where Oxman works, was stymied with what all these silkworms were for and how to process this in their accounting records since living organisms aren't considered construction materials. For Oxman, it didn't matter; this was part of what she needed to get her project done whether or not other departments understood it.

Netflix featured Oxman in its series *Abstract: The Art of Design*. This series highlights top designers in many fields and shows how they apply design skills in revolutionary ways. Oxman is quoted as being the embodiment of art, design, science, and engineering in a living human, so it's not surprising she starts the episode humorously brushing off the fact that nobody understands what she does.

"What question do you get the most?" an off-camera interviewer asks Oxman.

"What the hell do I do?" she replies with a slight chuckle.

Someone like Oxman is hard to classify. Who is she as a professional? What job title should she have? She is a professor, but that's not all. Being at the intersection of art, design, science, and engineering, she constantly crosses boundaries, meaning she does things that don't fit neatly into a box.

Oxman exemplifies a hybrid professional because she reconfigures known disciplines into new forms. She functions in the liminal space between them. Her work is interdisciplinary, transdisciplinary, and anti-disciplinary, all at the same time.

If you were Oxman, how would you introduce yourself or answer the question, what do you do? Oxman says she focuses on designing new materials "for, with, and by nature." Maybe a title like Nature Whisperer or Biomaterials Nymph might suit her, yet neither fully captures her artistic, architectural, biological, and ecological influences.

Perhaps the better question is what does Oxman want to call herself? What name does she want to give to her hybrid professional identity? The choice is really hers to make.

It's no small feat for hybrid professionals to effectively describe what they do. Vocabulary is insufficient and generic titles don't work. This is why, as a hybrid, you need to own your hybridity and invent your own job title. You can reframe, rethink, and rename who you are and what you want to be called.

The Job Title Trap

"Roles are changing faster than job titles can even reflect," wrote Sam Slaughter, founder of Lighthouse Creative Group, in 2015. At that time, Sam noticed a plethora of strange new job titles cropping up across companies and professionals. What was an influencer, or a culture hacker, or a story architect? he asked.

Look at job titles that exist today that didn't exist ten years ago: app developer, social media manager, Uber driver, cloud computing specialist, drone operator. Now, consider ten years from today. We can't predict the jobs of the future, nor can we predict the career paths to get there, but undoubtedly, many of them will be hybrid.

A cartoon in a 2015 *New York Times* article titled "Your Job Title Is…What?" made fun of job titles by labeling people and animals that were in the same living room scene. A delivery person stood in the doorway with the title *Expediter of Caloric Input*. A football player on the TV screen had the title *Fabricator, Department of Subdural Hematomas*. The cat scratching the couch was the *Director of Upholstery Restructuring*. The husband sitting on the couch was the *Overlord of Entertainment Infrastructure*. His wife, seated beside him, was the *Chief Gripe Officer*. The adolescent playing a video game on his laptop was the *Homework Avoidance Strategist*.

These titles are creative, to the point, and slightly offensive. Imagine actually calling a wife the Chief Gripe Officer. How do you imagine she'd respond?

Titles can be literal. Titles can be figurative. Titles can also be generic, or they can make you stop and think. Job titles shouldn't be overly confusing, flowery, trendy, obnoxious, or otherwise dense. They must be direct and digestible, finding a balance between cleverness and familiarity. New twists on old ideas or a refresh of traditional terms can be beneficial because, when done well, they can reveal different sides of us and our work and make us stand out.

In today's competitive workforce, professionals have to stand apart from the thousands of other people with similar job titles, backgrounds, and professional expertise. Professionals get lost in a sea of others with the same or similar job titles. On paper, professionals with the same title sound the same, even though they work for different companies and have different clients and responsibilities. Generic titles such as director of [department name], athlete, writer, coach, artist, or actor get you stereotyped. Without descriptive detail or other cues, there's nothing to help someone interpret more about you. Merely stringing professional identities together can make matters worse; more titles doesn't equal more clarity or more value.

Dilbert, the cartoon character, once struggled with his job title. He wanted a change, but got shot down and had to negotiate.

He approached Catbert, and the heading read, "Catbert: Evil Director of Human Resources."

Dilbert said, "I'd like to change my job title to something with 'architect' in it. My dream is to do less work while allegedly being more valuable."

Catbert replied, "The best I can do is 'code monkey.'"

Dilbert responded, "How about 'software simian?'"

Obviously, Dilbert's intentions for changing his job title were not sincere. Title inflation was a poor reason for a change of title request.

This comic strip shows that people can create titles for themselves, and people are assigned titles by others based on how they see the work they do. Job titles can be about power and hierarchy in organizations, yet workers can also craft job titles that better suit their professional identity. Hybrids can name their hybridity and use that name outside of or in addition to a job title they're assigned by an employer.

Are hybrids supposed to share one professional identity or job title, or should they share multiple identities or job titles when people ask them what they do? Why don't hybrids share their hybridity or hybrid job title?

The reason is simple: hybrids don't actually know what to call themselves. They've never thought to create a hybrid title for themselves.

Hybrid Professional Job Titles

Hybrid professional job titles aren't about coming up with the craziest, most off-the-wall, wild job title you can think of. It's a process of getting clear on your primary professional identities and then choosing a title that truly reflects the relationships between them. Don't depend on others to create your title, because it will never reflect your full value. Take the reins and design a title that defines who you are and market yourself as you want to be seen. You can use your hybrid job title as a secondary title, a personal title, in addition to formal job titles if you're in an organization or they can be your only title if you work for yourself.

If people don't know what to call you because you keep changing jobs or you wear a lot of hats, then you define your hybridity for the world—don't wait for the world to define it for you.

Your hybrid job title can run the gamut: a mashup of existing words, a phrase, an analogy, or a clever grouping of terms. One example of a mashup title is a hairipist, a combination of hairstylist and therapist. Another is a teacherpreneur, a teacher who teaches in the classroom but also leads work in the community. And another is a starchitect, an architect who creates designs for celebrities or a celebrity architect.

An example of a phrase is Jolly Good Fellow. That was the actual job title of Chade-Meng Tan when he worked at Google. Although he was an engineer, Tan focused on creating a mindfulness-based emotional intelligence course. Since he wasn't just an engineer, the title Jolly Good Fellow was better suited to his role and responsibilities.

David Clifford calls himself a serial edu-agitator because he brings an experience design and equity perspective to the field of education to agitate traditional systems. Chelley Canales calls herself a spiritual spark plug because she ignites inner awakening in her clients. Keren Nimmo calls herself a visionector because she thinks of herself as a master connector of people and a visionary. Brittany Sarconi calls herself the chief fire starter. Marcia Segall calls herself the Segall household chief sanity officer.

These hybrid titles are more dynamic, interesting, novel, thought-provoking, and accurate than traditional labels. In crafting these titles, professionals aren't trying to be cute or shorthanded. Rather, they're signifying the unique talents that result from the fusion of their professional identities. These titles express a full picture of who they are.

Introducing yourself as a hybrid and crafting your hybrid professional job title is an art. It's a fun process and there's no single right way to do it. It's not just about adding trendy buzzwords to your current title or calling yourself a sales guru or a coding wizard. Those are cheap ways of getting attention, but are not derived from the primary professional identities that make up your hybridity. Thoughtfulness and intentionality of word choice are a large part branding your hybrid professional identity.

If You Want to Find Your Hybrid Title, Think Outside of the Pizza Box

Creating a hybrid job title can be fun, but it also takes creative thinking. To start the process, it helps to be in a playful mood. Laughter and goofiness allow the brain to dream up uncommon ideas. The more you can break out of an analytical mindset, the easier new language will flow. It's best to brainstorm a number of wild possibilities before whittling it down to something that feels appropriate.

Figure 3. Think of crafting a hybrid job title the way you would name a bizarre flavor of pizza.

There are many tools you can use to craft a hybrid job title. I like to use professional identity math, which is about using the math operations of addition, subtraction, division, and multiplication, but doing it with identity words instead of numbers. You can add two words together to create a new word. You can take an idea and divide it into parts and call yourself a phrase. You can add adjectives and descriptive language to multiply the power of a word. You can modify or reduce a long title into something short and pithy. Professional identity math is a fun way of manipulating language to form a new identity.

Another tool is to think of crafting a hybrid job title the way you would name a bizarre flavor of pizza (Figure 3). When we use traditional names for pizza or call it by its parts, like the sausage and basil pizza or the spinach and feta pizza, we're at a straightforward, basic level that doesn't show off the uniqueness of how those ingredients taste together. But a title like Hawaiian pizza implies exoticness, and it's derived from the combination of its parts, pineapple and ham.

There's a pizza restaurant where I live called Boss Lady Pizza. They have a large array of specialty pizzas, which is why I love to go there. I order the Walter White, the Ricotta Be Kidding Me, or the Black and Blue Burger pizza because they're delicious and the names crack me up. And, that's the point. That's why they're specialty pizzas. The Walter White is a combination of a garlic and olive oil base, house-shredded mozzarella, a dash of salt, ricotta cheese, and their housemade seasoning.

No other pizza restaurant offers these hybrid combinations. When I read their menu, I think to myself, "There's no way that pizza tastes good. How do buffalo tater tots go with jalapenos and blue cheese on a pizza?" But, then I try it, and I'm blown away by how delicious it is. Reading a list of ingredients doesn't do a pizza justice. And a list of ingredients would make a really long name for a pizza if they didn't invent a hybrid name instead. Plus, eating pizza one ingredient at a time wouldn't taste the same as eating it all baked and melted together. The reason people love pizza is because the ingredients are combined into one. Hybrid professionals are like pizza. They are the sum of different identities in a special combination.

When professional identities integrate, that's when hybridity is formed. Think outside the pizza box when choosing your hybrid job title. Create one that uniquely describes what you do and that's based on your core professional identities. That will define the type of hybrid you are.

How to Introduce Yourself as a Hybrid

In her article "'Monochromatic' Job Titles Are Becoming Obsolete, or: Embracing Being a Hybrid," Kate Hamill talks about introducing herself:

> I have a hybrid career. I'm an actor/playwright/freelance writer—and I'm lucky to cobble together a living from all three. But something about saying that out loud at parties made me blush. It sounded, to my ears, a little bit flakey or unserious. The hybrid of three careers made me feel like I appeared un-invested, wishy-washy. It made me, uh, twitchy. But then, I started noticing something: the same thing was true of *so many* people around me. Slashes abounded everywhere I looked. Colleagues and friends were directors/teachers, designers/entrepreneurs, filmmakers/heads of marketing, writers/producers, nannies/photographers, programmers/painters, engineers/illustrators, accountants/activists.

Hamill isn't alone in her experience. It's daunting to introduce yourself as someone who does many things for work.

And, what she realized is that she shouldn't feel as though it made her sound wishy-washy because other people are in her shoes, too. A lot of people at networking events introduce themselves with multiple identities. The question is how to take that introduction to the next level and show the relationships between the identities to help others understand the power of the interconnectedness.

When Brian Corrigan told me he brings play into communities to do interactive placemaking and build social networks, I wondered, what job title would work for him? In his description of himself, Brian uses his designer background, community building expertise, gamification knowledge, and economic development skills. He probably wears three or four hats to do that work. If he called himself an economic development specialist that would reduce him to a single dimension of who he is, which inadequately represents his full professional identity.

Most hybrids introduce themselves awkwardly, trying to explain what they do on the spot in a way that makes sense for the other person. They boil themselves down to a few keywords, hoping it's the right summary, and it usually misses the elements of integration and connection of identities. That's what hybrids have to learn to do in their introductions. There's an easy method I'll share in a moment called the hybrid professional identity elevator pitch.

Today, Brian calls himself a creative strategist to encompass his hybridity. This means he "believes in the natural selection of ideas where crowds inform what assets are the strongest and then they optimize accordingly." This is a richer and clearer way for Brian to express who he is.

Declaring that you're a hybrid professional upfront in any introduction, email, or cover letter is the best tactic. It provides a cue that you possess multiple professional identities and that you blend them together. Likewise, the word *hybrid* acts as a primer because it signals a combination. Using the word hybrid in the opening sentence of an introduction makes the recipient curious to learn what type of hybrid you are. The term *hybrid* also generates a bit of intrigue and allows you to insert your own meaning and definition.

> "Instead of hoping your audience will know what you mean when you list the three, five, or ten things you do, a hybrid professional brands themselves, owns their hybridity, and defines the value for their audience, taking the guesswork out."

When I was figuring out how to articulate my hybrid identity, I tested it in a variety of professional settings. The reaction I was looking for was that professionals of all backgrounds quickly got it, and that it piqued their curiosity. Both criteria mattered to me. Additionally, I wanted to feel good when I shared my identity with others and confident when I said it aloud.

I wanted my identity to be a springboard to engage the other person and deepen our conversation, instead of coming across as familiar or forgettable. In the past, when I introduced myself using my traditional job title, the introductions felt flat, and the follow-up conversation was dull or nonexistent. Sure, some of this had to do with my lesser skills in networking back then or where I was in my career at the time. But even when I had more interesting roles and higher job titles, people still didn't understand what I did or what value I brought to my role. Using my hybrid professional identity became a better way to explain myself in the way I chose to define myself.

The Hybrid Professional Identity Elevator Pitch

The hybrid professional identity pitch is a framework for a ten-second script. Use it whenever you like, especially when someone asks what you do. I've found if I hit three specific talking points in order, then I eliminate a lot of the murkiness and guesswork for my listener. This sets a good foundation for the rest of the conversation. There are three parts to the hybrid professional identity elevator pitch:

First, state your name, and say that you are a hybrid professional. If you've developed a name for your hybrid professional identity, then share that too. It sounds like this, "I'm Sarabeth Berk, and I'm a hybrid professional. I call myself a creative disruptor."

This works for the opening line because you provide a new term, hybrid professional, which provokes curiosity and leaves the listener wanting more. If you add the name of your hybrid professional identity, that's even better, because you give the listener a new soundbite they've never heard before. It makes them even more curious.

The name of a strong hybrid professional identity sounds a little abstract and a little familiar so the listener almost gets what you mean but not fully. You don't want something that's ordinary but also not too bizarre. You want to strike a balance.

Second, explain the primary professional identities that inform your hybridity. These are the identities you use on a daily basis, that bring you joy, and that you want to be known for. It sounds like this, "I'm an artist, educator, researcher, and designer."

The reason you list these after you introduce yourself as a hybrid professional, and potentially after the name of your hybrid professional identity, is that it helps move from an abstract title to something more concrete. You need to define what makes you a hybrid by listing the ingredients that make up your hybridity. These are the identities that will be familiar for your listener.

Third, explain what you mean. Now you need to explain how your professional identities fit together. It sounds like this, "I creatively design systems to encourage people from different sectors to collaborate and build solutions."

This last part is the most important. Saying you're a hybrid professional and then listing your professional identities doesn't demonstrate what makes you a hybrid. The relationship between your professional identities is what makes you unique, so you need to define your uniqueness. The explanation of how your professional identities fit together and what you do with them is what sets you apart.

There's also a fourth step, but it's optional. If you have enough time or feel it would be beneficial, add a sentence about what purpose you're trying to achieve and what audience you serve or support. This provides more insight around your goals or vision—it's the *why* behind what you do.

When you string the three parts together, the full introduction sounds something like this:

"Hi, nice to meet you. I'm Sarabeth Berk, and I'm a hybrid professional. I call myself a creative disruptor. This means I use my artist, educator, researcher, and designer identities to creatively design systems to encourage people from different sectors to collaborate and build solutions."

Try this three- or four-part framework the next time you're networking and trying to express the value of your hybrid professional identity.

You Know You've Landed at the Right Hybrid Professional Title When...

After you've developed a hybrid professional title, then it's time to test it in public to see how others respond to it. You may not get the reaction you want the first time, or the first few times. Be patient and persistent. Test it in low-risk situations first, with people you know, not total strangers, so you can get feedback and learn what didn't make sense or what words they think you should change. This process should incite playfulness and curiosity as you investigate the fit and effectiveness of your identity.

I knew I found my stride in being seen as a hybrid professional when my boss introduced me to a new colleague like this, "This is Sarabeth Berk. She's a hybrid. She has an artist, researcher, and educator background, which is why she's great at leading this initiative." Hearing this shocked me. It was the first time I had heard another person introduce me as a hybrid, and it revealed that other people saw me the way I saw myself, and they saw the value in it. It felt good to hear my boss say this about me because it legitimized that she believed in my hybridity.

It was also interesting to hear the way she introduced me. Even though she didn't use my title of creative disruptor, that didn't matter. She saw my hybridity, she articulated my primary identities, and she explained how she saw that as important to the work I did for her and the organization.

Later, in a different role, a different boss came up to me one day and asked me, "How are you doing in the job? Do you feel like you're getting to use all your different identities?" Again, I had never heard a boss say that to me before. The fact that she asked that question showed me she understood my hybridity and how using my professional identities in tandem mattered to me.

You'll know you've found your stride in sharing your hybrid professional identity when other people start reflecting it back to you. They'll see you the way you want to be seen. These moments with my two bosses were important because they showed me that I had done a good job of shaping my professional identity, and it was sticking. When other people can articulate or comment on your hybridity in positive ways, you'll know they get you. Being celebrated for your hybridity in the workplace is when you know others understand that your hybridity is a great asset.

KEY IDEAS ABOUT HYBRID PROFESSIONALS

- Use the phrase "I'm a hybrid professional," along with your formal job title, during an introduction. This will spark intrigue and invite deeper questions about what that means.

- Create your own hybrid professional job title. You get to name your hybridity. This title will always be with you no matter the other formal job titles you hold, or if you're between jobs.

- Design a hybrid title that's unique but not too obscure or trendy. It should differentiate you from your colleagues and competitors and reveal your value. Update it as often as you like.

- Get familiar with the hybrid professional identity elevator pitch. State your name, followed by your title, and then list your two or three professional identities that form your hybridity. If you have time, give a one sentence explanation of how your identities connect and why that makes you unique.

PART TWO

The Path Toward Hybrid Professional Identity

Getting Clear on Identity and Professional Identity

"I don't like trends. They tend to make everybody look the same."

—**Carolina Herrera,** *Venezuelan fashion designer*

WHEN BRENÉ BROWN, A renowned researcher of shame and vulnerability, is asked what she does, even she struggles to answer. In her book *The Gifts of Imperfection*, Brown wrote, "I used to wince every time someone asked me this question." Then, she explained:

> I felt like my choices were to reduce myself to an easily digestible sound bite or to confuse the hell out of people. Now my answer to "What do you do?" is, "How much time do you have?" Most of us have complicated answers to this question. For example, I'm a mom, partner, researcher, writer, storyteller, sister, friend, daughter, and teacher. All of these things make up who I am, so I never

know how to answer that question, and to be honest with you, I'm tired of choosing to make it easier on the person who asked.

Can You Relate?

Look at what's happening in Brown's statement. She lists an array of identities: some are professional (researcher, writer, teacher), while others are social or familial (friend, mother, daughter). Brown illustrates that she has nine different identities, and this is why it's difficult to quickly or simply answer the what do you do question. Explaining nine different identities takes time, and that's not even her full list.

Yet, when people ask what you do, they want a short, sweet, easy-to-digest nugget that gives a snapshot of who you are. That feels like a tall order. To Brown's point, maybe the better response is to answer with how much time do you have?

Identity is not a straightforward thing. It's a social construct that comprises lots of different parts. From personal to professional identities and beyond, there are many kinds of identities. I want to take a moment to acknowledge this and discuss identity versus professional identity. It's important to see how the two concepts are interconnected and how they're separate.

Our identities show up in different ways on different days and in different combinations depending on the situation or the stage of life we're in. Every time we're asked what we do, we evaluate the context and audience to decide how to respond. We mentally ask ourselves which identities we should share and why. It's an exhausting and complicated mental exercise.

Identity, in its simplest terms, is how we define oursel-ves. It's who we believe we are and what characteristics and components make us *us*. Identity research looks at how identities can remain fixed while others are fluid, contex-tual, and dynamic. Some identities stay the same and others evolve over the course of our lifetimes.

Identity Is A Social Construct

Dan Gilbert, a professor of psychology at Harvard, studies why we make decisions that our future selves regret. He talks about how we get tattoos in our twenties, and then ten years later, we get those tattoos removed because we no longer like them or think they're cool. Gilbert teasingly phrases this as, "that tattoo simply isn't 'us' anymore."

Getting a tattoo, and then getting it removed, is an example of how our identity changes over time. In our twenties, we can't imagine that our tastes in clothes, music, friends, or geography will change, but they do. We perceive that we'll stay the same in the future. But later, upon reflec-tion and looking at old photos of ourselves, we see how much we've really changed.

That's not to say our entire identity changes. Some identities remain stable and fixed. These typically include race, socioeconomic status, gender, ability, sexual orien-tation, religion, nationality, and ethnicity. These are the most common socially constructed identities. Researchers frequently use these to compare and contrast the lived experiences of groups of people, especially in terms of privilege and oppression. You've probably seen check boxes for these identities on surveys and applications because they're a primary form of collected identity data.

Besides the most common identities, there are other types. These include but are not limited to education, relationship status, hobbies, geography, age, language, intelligence, and profession. You can see how long this list can grow in terms of all the possible identities you can have. The more groups you're part of—whether that's being a member of an organization, joining a club, being on a board, or playing on a team—the more identities you have. One person can associate with or have dozens of identities. Which identities you choose to share when you meet someone new or introduce yourself is always a bit of a guessing game and a gamble.

I've found that sometimes it's the identities I reveal later in a conversation or by accident that have the most impact. Of course, there's no way I would have known to lead with those identities, which is why it's tricky to choose a few identities to share in the first moments of an encounter. For instance, when I met my new boss, he wanted to know about my past professional identities and former jobs, so I led with that. At one point, we shifted to talking about hometowns and hobbies, and that's where we learned we both were skiers and had grown up in rural ski towns. That opened up a new level of connection between us, but it wasn't where we started.

Identity can account for personal constructions, social constructions, or constructions that are discovered over time. Carol Rodgers and Katherine Scott argue that contemporary conceptions of identity pertain to four areas, which include the notions that identity is dependent and formed from multiple contexts, identity is formed through relations with others, identity is constantly shifting and multiple, and identity is about constructing meaning through stories.

Because identity is complex and varied, it's hard to see all the different sides of one person from the outset. Every time we meet someone new, we're determining what parts of ourselves to share first, and what to reveal later. Keep in mind that people have dozens of identities.

Perceived, Assigned, and Projected Identities

Another element of identity research is perceived identities, assigned identities, and projected identities. Perceived identities are ones that you or other people believe you have. Assigned identities are the ones people give to you. Projected identities are ones you choose to present to the world.

Identities can also be achieved or ascribed. Achieved identities are those you accomplish on your own, perhaps by earning a degree or getting a promotion. Ascribed identities are those you're born into or inherit, such as race, class, and nationality.

Sometimes perceived, assigned, and projected identities are the same, and other times they're not. For instance, at one point in my career, I was assigned the identity of teacher, and for a while, that's what I was. I openly promoted that title to my peers, colleagues, and new acquaintances.

As I grew in my abilities and my career goals shifted, I saw myself as more than a teacher. My artist and researcher identities were becoming stronger and more visible. I was making and selling art and learning how to study big ideas by collecting evidence. I wanted to project that I had other professional identities beyond being a teacher, but the world didn't see me that way. At that stage in my career, there was a mismatch between what I perceived my professional identities were, and what the world assigned to me.

When these mismatches occur, it's challenging to be seen as the person you think you are. Shifting how others see you becomes the hurdle. As you evolve, and your identities evolve, outside perceptions also have to evolve, and this takes time. It's a process.

This mismatch between your perceptions of yourself versus how others perceive you or what they assign to you is notable in professional identity. When professional identity changes, it's more pronounced than other identities. While becoming a parent or getting married are both major identity shifts, they happen less frequently over the course of a lifetime than getting a new job. The average person holds more than ten jobs in a lifetime and reshapes their career three to four times, according to John Hagel at Wharton. That's a lot of professional identity shifting.

You Can Only Juggle a Few Identities at a Time

To recap, first, identity is how we define ourselves. Second, people possess many types of identities, and these can be fixed or dynamic, changing over our lifetime. Third, identity can be perceived, assigned, and projected.

The last important point is that identities do not appear all at the same time. Imagine if you went around being all of your identities at once—how crazy would that be?

Although we possess dozens of identities, we only have capacity to use or manage a few at any given time. To accommodate this, some identities become prominent while others diminish. This is why certain identities show up more when you're at work than when you're at home or out with friends.

As a result, we shift between identities. Research doesn't have an exact number of how many identities people can maintain at once, and it's different for each person, but it's safe to say most people can handle a few, maybe two or three, at a time. Since we're accustomed to shifting back and forth as needed, it might even look like more.

This dance of shifting between identities and evolving from one identity into another is human nature. We are identity jugglers, chameleons, and shapeshifters. We know how to hold space for different identities to coexist within us simultaneously. This is how we accommodate being a parent, a husband, a musician, an executive, a swimmer, and a wine connoisseur. This is what makes us *us*. We have multiple identities that fit together into our full identity.

Professional Identity

"Professional identity is anything you do that you consider to be your work, whether you get paid for it."

In the U.S., when workers lose a job or feel lost in their careers, their self-esteem is affected because higher self-worth is connected to a stronger sense of professional identity. A person's overall identity suffers without the clarity of their professional identity. For this reason, professional identity carries a lot of weight for most Americans. Importantly, this is not necessarily the same in other countries, where cultural values and norms around work and professional identity differ.

Professional identity is one among a spectrum of identities. So, it follows the same principles that pertain to identity theory. Professional identity can remain the same or be fluid, contextual, and dynamic. It can also be perceived, assigned, or projected.

I define professional identity as anything you consider to be your work, whether or not you get paid for it. This means that if you consider a volunteer role or an unpaid internship to be part of your work, then that qualifies as one of your professional identities. A hobby or something you do as a pastime is not a professional identity because that's not your work, it's fun, and it should remain fun and not be work.

If you work, then you have a professional identity. If you're retired from working or not currently working, you may still consider that you have a professional identity. If you do more than one thing for work—have multiple jobs, freelance or consult, or have multiple roles within one organization—then you might have multiple professional identities.

This is where professional identity research gets interesting. How can you have more than one professional identity at the same stage of life?

Think of identity as a pie. Each pie slice represents a different identity. One slice is your professional identity. What happens if you cut that slice into even more slices? Are you allowed to do that? How does that work? What happens?

These are the questions I study. Among my professional identities, I'm a researcher of professional identity, and I specifically focus on hybrid professional identity and hybrid professionals. I don't consider myself to be an identity researcher because identity research is a massive field that's complex unto itself.

Instead, I investigate how people experience their professional identity. In the new economy, old norms of professional identity are being altered and questioned, and new forms are emerging. I'm very intrigued by this and few researchers are studying it.

Other identities certainly weave into professional identity, like being a parent or an athlete, but to hold a tight research scope, I only study professional identity in relation to other professional identities. If you're a person for whom religion or being a parent or some other identity really matters to your professional identity, then that's important for you to know about yourself, but for the scope of this work, I have not analyzed those connections.

KEY IDEAS ABOUT HYBRID PROFESSIONALS

- Define yourself and who you think you are. That's what your identity is.

- Accept that as you change, so does your identity. Identities can be fixed for the duration of your lifetime, or fluid and dynamic, changing with time, age, and the situation.

- Realize there are perceived, assigned, and projected identities that affect how others see you and how you see yourself.

- Know that we can only manage a few identities at once, but we are good at shifting between many. We can promote them or suppress them depending on what's happening in a moment.

- Understand that professional identity is one of our main identities because we use it so much, and it represents anything you do that you consider to be your work, whether you get paid. But, it is not a hobby.

CHAPTER 5

Three Types of Identity: Singularity, Multiplicity, Hybridity

"Binaries aside, we are the products of our relationships with our identities—cities we have built, bodies we have embraced, kindred souls we've cherished, our memories, our dreams, the fears we hide, the pain we hold— identities that cannot be reduced to a collection of labels."

Neri Oxman, American–Israeli designer and professor at the MIT Media Lab

OF ALL OUR DIFFERENT identities, professional identity plays a major role in our self-worth and self-confidence. Society has conditioned us that our reputation is defined by what we do, which is typically correlated to our occupation and job title. Expanding definitions of professional identity, to be more than either an expert or a generalist, is critical to helping us make sense of who we are in our professional lives.

Professional identity is a spectrum, although it appears to be binary. It's a myth that you're either an expert or a generalist, because there are people who are expert-generalists. These ideas fall into three types of professional identity: *singularity, multiplicity,* and *hybridity.*

You may have been taught that professional identity is an either/or decision—you can either be a scientist or a musician. Or, you may believe you're only allowed to have one identity at a time. But that's not the case. There are professionals who are both/and, meaning they are a scientist/musician combo. They are deeply talented in more than one discipline, or perhaps they're a hyperspecialist in one topic and a generalist in many others. Their degree of knowledge and experience across domains may vary, but they bring together skills from disparate spaces.

IllMind (his professional name) is known as a sound design pioneer because he makes fresh beats and sounds by mixing his producer, designer and musician identities. Yet, he's not a producer, a designer or a musician one at a time. He's not a multipotentialite or a polymath. He integrates his identities. As a result, IllMind manipulates snippets of different sounds from instruments like snares, drums, and tambourines to create original beats that are later sold and recorded behind popular music tracks.

Likewise, Jad Abumrad is known as a sound scientist and the co-host of the popular radio show *Radiolab.* Jad isn't just a writer or a musician. He's both. He's a sound scientist because, like IllMind, he manipulates sounds into complex audio for Radiolab. They say his home studio is the audio equivalent of a sketchbook.

IllMind and Abumrad both call themselves musicians. They have expertise and passion in music. They are also talented in other areas like writing or sound production. They obviously have multiple professional identities. This means they could introduce themselves by one of their professional identities or by all of them. Yet, neither scenario does justice to who they really are.

IllMind and Abumrad are hybrid professionals. They have hybrid job titles of sound design pioneer and sound scientist, respectively, reflecting the new ways they work and the new value they bring as professionals. Although they both produce beats, they don't do it in the same style or in the same way. Hybridity is where uniqueness comes alive.

IllMind and Abumrad have one professional identity. They also have multiple professional identities. More importantly, they are a combination of their professional identities that are formed at the intersections of their other identities. That's a new type of professional identity, a hybrid professional identity.

As I discussed earlier, some of our identities can be fluid and contextual and change over time, while others, like being a sister, are fixed and can last a lifetime. People have multiple identities simultaneously, but in work, we reduce people to one professional identity, or sometimes even one identity at a time. We have a tendency to define the professional identity of workers as experts or generalists instead of hybrids.

I'm sure you know professionals who shift between professional identities, and this may even be the case for you. Ask yourself this question: What were you doing ten years ago? Is it the same work you're doing today, or has your professional identity evolved into something else?

Whether from moment to moment or year to year, you may suddenly perform different tasks. You might be an event planner, then a few minutes later the website designer, and then an hour later the photographer for the event. Or you might be a small business consultant, and then a few years later become a real estate agent. Shifting professional identities can span a lifetime, in big career shifts, or within a company, where you get promoted or even wear multiple hats within a single role.

The popular belief is you must be good at one thing—you must be a deep expert in something because generalists dabble and aren't valued in the same way. Their skill set is more common, and let's be honest, more easily replaceable. Society wants to define us by our professional identity, emphasizing having one primary professional identity or at the very least, only using one identity at a time to get the job done.

For workers like me, who like to do or are good at doing multiple things, the model until now has been to choose one of two options. The first option is I can share only one thing I do. That way, I look focused to an audience but they don't see the diversity of my talents. The second option is I can list all the things I do, which showcases my different abilities but also risks confusing my audience about what I'm best at. Both tactics minimize who I am and what I offer the workforce. It's nonsense that I have to hide my different professional identities because I might scare away employers or clients in fear that they won't know what to hire me for. Today, I look for roles where I'm allowed to be my full professional self so I can deliver maximum value for a client or a job. I feel my best when I can use all of my abilities together.

On the professional identity spectrum, we haven't had a term to describe people who are between singularity and multiplicity. We need a common term to describe professionals whose professional identities intersect, like a Venn diagram. As discussed previously, this new type of professional identity is hybridity.

The Three Types of Professional Identity

All three types of professional identity— singularity, multiplicity, and hybridity—are important in the workforce. No one type is better than another, they're just different ways people show up and do their work. We need all three because they serve different purposes. Having an awareness that three different types exist helps us better understand what type of worker a person is. This way, we can make sense of a person's professional identity and work style. A professional who is a deep expert in a topic will work differently and need different things in their job than someone who wears multiple hats or a hybrid who combines them all.

It's difficult to estimate how many people fall into each type of professional identity since there's no good data on this, so I can't provide a proportion of workers among the three types, but I doubt it's an even spread. Since everyone has at least one professional identity, it's obvious that the entire workforce meets the category of singularity. If people have more than one job or if they shift careers, then they likely fall into multiplicity and this captures much of the workforce too.

Here's an overview of the three types of professional identity. There is a graphic illustration of these in chapter 2.

Singularity

Professionals who only do one thing or only have one professional identity fall into the singularity type. Someone of this type might be an expert for a period of time in one position, wholly focused on one domain, or specialize in one area for the duration of their career. People who know what they want to be when they grow up and remain in that career until they retire fall into singularity.

Certain jobs require deep focus, advanced skills, specific knowledge, or repetitive execution by trained individuals. People who know how to do complex data entry, operate robots, perform brain surgery, engineer highways, play piano concertos, or create monumental glass sculptures are examples of singularity. It takes years of training and practice to become great at something and have deep knowledge of it, or people may like their job and stick with it for years, even if it doesn't require deep knowledge.

Multiplicity

Professionals who are good at many things or can do many things for work fall into multiplicity. This could be someone who has a range of responsibilities in one role even though they only have one job title, a freelancer who manages different clients and projects, or a person who has many jobs or careers over a lifetime. Multiplicity is about many. People who list a series of professional identities like "author, spokesperson, head of sales, and founder of Project X" beside their name or in their introductions demonstrate multiplicity.

Profile headers in LinkedIn are a perfect illustration of where multiplicity appears. Many professionals use a variety of punctuation such as commas, slashes, hyphens, ampersands, dashes, and other symbols to portray multiplicity. Professionals with multiplicity also tend to have multiple business cards, that way they can hand out the right card with the right audience, or they have multiple titles listed on one business card. There is no one way or right way to display multiple identities, and the flexible nature of how this is being done in profile headers and on business cards is fascinating to observe.

The key thing to remember about professionals of this type is that they do a lot of things for work, but they only do one thing at a time. There's no overlap between their roles or professional identities. Separation exists between their identities.

Hybridity

Professionals who integrate multiple professional identities and work from the intersections of those identities fall into the category of hybridity. It's no longer sufficient in the new economy to think the opposite of singularity means multiplicity. The third option that's missing is hybridity.

Although singularity typically refers to experts and multiplicity typically refers to generalists, hybrids are more than expert-generalists. Hybrids have deep expertise, and they have general knowledge, so don't stereotype the ratio of what they bring together. They have their own hybrid combination of experience and skills.

Hybrid professionals must have at least two professional identities, since two identities create one intersection, the space where hybridity exists. It's in those intersections where hybrid professionals integrate skills, knowledge, experience, and disciplines. I've devoted Chapter 7 to discussing what happens in the intersections because it's that important and there's so much to share.

Two distinguishing factors that separate hybridity from multiplicity are *integration* and *interrelationships of professional identities*. For instance, I met a financial advisor who used to be an airline pilot. She told me that as a pilot, she was trained to follow practice, procedure, and gut—that was her mantra. Now that she was a financial advisor, that same mantra was part of how she approached financial advising, because it was ingrained in her work ethic. How many other financial advisors would talk about flying airplanes as part of how they approach their advising work? That's one example of how hybridity shows up.

For a hybrid professional to communicate who they are, they have to make sense of how two or more of their professional identities merge, and it's unique for each hybrid. Not all professional identities overlap well to produce value, and that's okay. Just because a person has multiple professional identities doesn't mean those identities blend perfectly together or even all the time; some identities may and others may not. A hybrid has to figure out their sweet spot by sensing the strength and power of the connections between their different identities. That's how they leverage the potential of their intersections.

Hybrid professionals don't have to work in their intersections all the time, and in fact, staying in the intersectional space isn't always easy, especially for emerging hybrids. Hybrids may move in and out of their intersections, both at will and by chance. There are a variety of reasons for this, mostly based on circumstances and how adept a hybrid professional is at navigating their intersections.

The option to use only one professional identity versus working at the intersections of their professional identities is never off-limits for hybrids. If they need to shift from hybridity to multiplicity, it doesn't mean they're no longer a hybrid, it's usually a temporary change. Hybrids find their peak performance and highest sense of job satisfaction and engagement when they work from their intersections, so hybrids naturally gravitate back to their intersections. Since working in the intersections is enjoyable and pleasurable, hybrids want to work from that space as much as possible.

In fact, when hybrids isolate their identities and only use one—whether they're on a project that requires it, a boss tells them to, or a client has requested it—after a period of time (could be days, weeks, or longer depending on the individual), a hybrid will grow uncomfortable and dissatisfied. Outwardly, they'll appear restless and frustrated because they thrive when they blend their identities together.

Asking hybrid professionals to only use a portion of their professional identities is like asking them to work with one hand tied behind their back. They can do it for a short period but after a while, they need their hand back. Without it, they're not their full selves, and they're not working at their highest and best ability. When hybrids get to hybridize, meaning they get to fully utilize all of their abilities, that's when they perform exceptional feats, drive new value, and deliver types of work that defies labels and titles.

- Know where you fall in the three types of professional identity: singularity, multiplicity, and hybridity.

- Note the difference between multiplicity and hybridity. Hybridity is about integration and interrelationships of professional identities.

- Using one identity at a time is singularity or multiplicity.

- Feeling restless and frustrated happens to hybrids when they're asked to work within a single identity.

CHAPTER 6

Developing Hybrid Professional Identity

"Put your efforts toward the things that are important to you and that you do best, the things that only you can do."
—*Veronica Corzo-Duchart, graphic designer/artist*

WHEN PROFESSIONALS APPROACH ME and tell me they're hybrid professionals, their initial comment is often something like this: "I do a lot of things for work. I didn't know it, but I'm a hybrid."

As we talk, and I get to know them better, it becomes clear that they're not actually a hybrid professional. Instead, they're what I call an *emerging hybrid,* rather than a fully developed hybrid professional.

Emerging Hybrid Professional	Fully Developed Hybrid Professional
Doesn't know their primary professional identities	Clearly knows their primary professional identities
Struggles to find their sweet spot (what they do in their intersections)	Has found their sweet spot and is familiar with their intersections
Has to concentrate to cross over between professional identities	Unconsciously and effortlessly crosses over between professional identities
Doesn't know what their intersections are or can't articulate what happens when they're in them	May or may not be able to articulate what happens in their intersections but knows how it feels when they're in them
Doesn't know when they're in flow, or has ad hoc feelings of flow in their work; stumbles into flow by accident	Knows when they're in flow and how to enter flow in their work; can get there on purpose
Talks about and thinks about professional identities as parts of themselves	Talks about and thinks about professional identities as a mixture
Doesn't see or can't express the connections or relationships between their different professional identities	Can immediately express the connections and relationships between their different identities
Delivers a confusing introduction or elevator pitch of who they are, what they do for work, and why that matters	Delivers a unique, compelling, clear, and concise introduction or elevator pitch of who they are, what they do for work, and why that matters

Figure 4. Key differences between emerging and fully developed hybrids.

Figure 4 demonstrates the key differences between emerging and fully developed hybrids. With insights like those you're learning in this book, tools, and practice, emerging hybrids can learn how to embrace and further develop their hybridity.

Becoming a hybrid professional isn't necessarily automatic or inevitable. After studying professional identity, it's apparent that some people evolve into hybridity naturally, even unconsciously, while others need coaching and guidance to get there if they're on that path already. Hybridity can be learned, and some people are more inclined to it than others. That's why there are different types of professional identity and different types of workers. Each person has a professional identity type that works for them.

If you're interested in becoming a hybrid professional, there are three critical factors that matter. Workers can become hybrids at different ages or stages of their careers, depending on where they are across these three factors. The first factor is developmental, as related to years of experience in the workforce as well as to human development. The second is awareness, as in how to work from your intersections and cross professional identities together. The third is self-confidence because you have to own and believe in the value of your hybridity. If you don't leverage your hybrid skill set, no one else will either.

Emerging Hybrids

When an emerging hybrid senses their hybridity, it's a time in their life when they're trying to discern how to apply all their talents together. They're usually frustrated or disheartened in their career. They're likely looking for a new job, and want to find work that will allow them to use all their skills more effectively. If they run their own business, emerging hybrids might consider new services to offer clients, how to expand their scope of work, or ways to evolve their business model. There's an antsy-ness, an itchiness, a frustration level, a desire for change I hear in the voices of professionals who are at the emerging hybrid stage.

At this stage, emerging hybrids usually enter a career transition as they feel ready to grow and expand in their professional identity. They can't put a finger on who they're becoming or what type of new role they're seeking because they don't know what to call themselves. Their professional identity is murky and all over the place. If you ask them to tell you who they are and what they do for work, they sound a lot like an "everything sandwich."

Even if they come across as confident and clear, they're actually not as clear as they think they are. I know this because I've interviewed many emerging hybrids, and while some sound like they know their primary professional identities, they typically still have more work to do. They're like a faulty electrical switch, causing the house lights to flicker intermittently—somewhere there's a loose wire and they're stuck until they figure out how to fix it. Conversely, fully developed hybrids are like a house that's all lit up and glowing, literally and figuratively. That's what hybrids are aiming for.

Emerging hybrids look like they're dabbling in their identities. Occasionally their hybridity comes out, but it's brief. They don't understand it well enough to maintain it consistently. They revert to multiplicity as their default operating state while they strive to become hybrids. They like what hybridity feels like when they're in it, but they don't know how to remain there. They're not even sure how they got there, so they're definitely not sure how to return. This is because they're not conscious of how they're integrating their different professional identities, which is why they slip out. Also, emerging hybrids are likely in a role or job that's restrictive and holding them back from being a hybrid more permanently.

I had a conversation with a professional named Joel Davis at a point in his life when he was struggling to find his hybrid identity. Joel calls himself the Vibrarian because he's more than a DJ. He's adept at drawing from a deep well of music and finding the right sound for any setting.

You might say Joel is a master of many parts of the music industry, since that's his passion, and, as a result, he's journeyed deep down that rabbit hole. Joel had his own record label, but he didn't enjoy the marketing side. He had a web platform with curated content, but he wasn't getting enough user traffic to sustain it. At the end of the day, what Joel truly enjoyed was being in the studio with the artist or sharing their music through his long-running weekly radio show, more than the day-to-day operations.

"I know my taste in music is as good as theirs," Joel told me when comparing his work to leading professionals in the music world, "but maybe I didn't have the right platform or confidence to get out there and sell myself." When I met Joel, he was the Resident DJ at a software development company, and it was the first time he felt appreciated for his multiple talents. Changing work environments and being in an office where he could select music for people in a live setting was a breath of fresh air. "For 20 years, no one noticed or appreciated my taste. Finally, someone appreciates it. It's given me more confidence to step into this role, and to own it, even though I'm still kind of shy about it." In that comment, Joel proves he's finally crossing and connecting his professional identities because he talks about how he feels different. He's sensing how his identities are coming together in new ways—a key part of being a full hybrid.

Emerging hybrids have to focus on developing a heightened sensitivity about the way they work. They also need to pay close attention to when they feel their best in their work. This means gaining more self-awareness so they're better able to recognize and describe what happens in their intersections.

Before moving on, I want to point out two specific areas where hybrid professionals struggle the most, especially those in the emerging stage. Having an idea of these upfront will help you see why I'm spending more time explaining them, and why it's necessary to devote extra time and attention to these aspects later in the book. When people gloss over these two elements or take them for granted, they're not able to figure out their hybridity.

The first area of struggle is getting clear on your primary professional identities. Once you know the two to four primary professional identities you use most frequently, the next area of struggle is how to crossover between them. It's easy to assume it's common sense and natural to blend identities together, but from what I've observed, this isn't always easy for professionals to do, especially in organizations (like large corporations) where roles are traditional and so are organizational charts and HR structures. You can't bounce from one professional identity to the next and expect hybridization to occur by happenstance. This is where professionals with multiplicity and those with hybridity are drastically different.

Imagine taking a bite from a plum and then taking a bite from an apricot and chewing them at the same time and telling people you're eating a pluot. Or using a spoon and a fork at the same time and saying you're using a spork. You're not. You're not eating a pluot or using a spork. That's multiplicity faking hybridity. A pluot is its own kind of fruit, a new fruit, and it's genetically different. And a spork is its own type of utensil. The spoon and fork are inseparable. Emerging hybrids have to release the mindset and behaviors of multiplicity and start to integrate their identities to become a fully developed hybrid professional.

Developing Hybridity

When I started studying professional identity, I became interested in the work of Robert Kegan, a constructivist and developmental psychologist at Harvard. Kegan expanded on the developmental theories of Piaget, Kohlberg, Maslow, and Erikson, and in 1982, he published a book called *The Evolving Self*. In it, Kegan articulates a framework that builds on his predecessors and describes his view of how humans make meaning of their human development and explore their inner experiences. He discusses how consciousness evolves and leads to a greater understanding of the world as we grow up, which factors into the development of hybrid professional identity.

In the introduction of *The Evolving Self*, Kegan described himself as a teacher, therapist, and researcher-theorist. Then, in his next book, *In Over Our Heads*, he wrote, "My core professional identity is that of teacher. Although this book draws on my experiences as a researcher, a theorist, a therapist, a director of an institute on lifelong education, and a consultant to work, life and professional development." Kegan was a leading theorist who influenced my research and is clearly a hybrid professional; through his own description of himself, he shows how his hybridity has helped him to do the research he's become famous for.

To summarize Kegan's work, he developed five orders of consciousness (Figure 5). This was his way of explaining how humans evolve in their understanding of themselves and of the world as they mature. Each order of consciousness represents a greater amount of consciousness that has to be achieved.

The first order starts when we're babies. We see the world in categories or single points of view. We attain the second order as we grow and develop. From about six years old into adolescence, we start to see cause and effect between objects and how one object affects another. By post-adolescence, we reach the third order, seeing beyond cause and effect and moving into understanding that there are mutual connections between things. The fourth and fifth orders of consciousness are about seeing the world as systems and not just parts or categories.

Not everyone reaches the fourth or fifth orders. According to Kegan, few adults reach the fourth order of consciousness, and only a small fraction reach the fifth order. Most adults attain the third order of consciousness and remain there for the duration of their lives. That means fewer adults are able to perceive the world from a systems view, or a systems of systems view. That's a very high level of consciousness.

Order of Consciousness	Psychological Growth & Development	Age
First Order	"Single Point Perceptions:" Fantasy, movement of object, impulses	Typically, 2 through 6 years old
Second Order	"Concrete Categories:" actuality, cause and effect, simple reciprocity	6 years old through adolescence
Third Order	"Cross-Categorical Abstractions:" Generalizations, role consciousness, mutual reciprocity	Post adolescence
Fourth Order	"Systems:" Multiple-role consciousness, ability to regulate and create (rather than be created by) our values and ideals, self-authorship	Variable, if achieved
Fifth Order	"Systems of Systems:" Self-transforming, dialectic between ideologies	Typically, over 40 years old, if achieved

[Figure 5. Adapted from Kegan's Orders of Consciousness]

The development of our professional identity mirrors the development of our consciousness. When we're young, in post-adolescence, our professional identities are greatly influenced and defined by how others see us and how we think we're supposed to act rather than how we perceive ourselves and who we want to be as professionals. This is because our consciousness is still at a stage where we're self-conscious and we idealize who we're supposed to be.

In post-adolescence, we build interpersonal relationships and notice how our relationships to desires and interests affect our work. Kegan considers this to be third-order consciousness, which is a focus between "what I am doing" and "what they expect me to do."

In fourth-order consciousness, which typically occurs in adulthood before forty years of age, professionals have a strong sense of self-authorship and individuation in how they do their work. The main difference between the third and fourth-order consciousness is that professionals who reach the fourth order can perceive the role they are supposed to play and faithfully adhere to it, but also understand that they can play a part in the actual creation and regulation of their role.

Professionals who reach the fifth order of consciousness are people who bring a *trans-system* or *cross-form* way of organizing reality. This means they can experience, in Kegan's words, multipleness. They see themselves as part of systems that interact and share with other systems. Kegan remarks that fifth-order consciousness is the "recognition of our multiple selves."

Professionals who reach this fifth order of consciousness rarely give a damn about how they work. This outcome is reminiscent of Neri Oxman's story I shared in Chapter 3. They just do what they do while still meeting expectations demanded of them. This mindset isn't coming from an attitude of disrespect or rebelliousness; rather these professionals are versatile in achieving outcomes by following their hybrid methods as opposed to the conventional standards set forth by one professional identity.

When I interviewed Brian Corrigan about his experience of developing hybridity, he said it felt like becoming a fully blossomed person. He described it this way: "The expert. That's what we call someone who has fully bloomed. There's so much tension before we open, but think of how good it feels to be fully opened." He went on to share that, just like a flowering plant, hybrids have professional identities that are like buds trying to come into being. Emerging hybrids are not fully blossomed and we all have different timing and different ways of blossoming.

My favorite point that Brian made was about the tension that happens before hybrids finally bloom. There's that incredible tension when hybrids are trying to be seen and to see themselves fully, and to figure out how it's all going to happen. Then, there's an amazing release when hybrids finally realize who they are. We can see them for their accomplishments and abilities, and the various parts of their professional selves finally come together.

I provided Brian's reflections and Kegan's theoretical context because it relates to the development of professional identity and moving from having multiple professional identities to having a hybrid professional identity. Development has to do with our readiness to bloom and awareness of how we work as professionals. Developing hybridity is about more than connecting multiple identities. There are developmental stages people must move through to allow them to reorganize reality and perceive how their professional identities are part of bigger systems and multipleness.

Although evolving consciousness to grow our understanding of ourselves and what we do for work may sound complex, we can break the concept of developing hybridity into bite-sized pieces, starting with primary professional identities. It's critical to acknowledge how sophisticated a process it is to realize your hybridity, which is why it isn't something you sit down to do in one afternoon or because you thought it would be fun to figure out. Becoming a hybrid professional is about raising your self-consciousness and doing deep self-reflection. This is what it takes to make sense of how you work in the world and what role you play in the workforce. Hybrids don't just do more work or balance professional identities better than other workers, they work in-between, and that's a sophisticated space of interconnectedness. It's also a radical way of thinking and talking about how certain workers perform their tasks.

Primary Professional Identities

First, figure out your primary identities. I classify professional identities into two kinds: primary versus non-primary. In reality, nonprimary is my shorthand for saying any identity that's secondary, tertiary, and so forth. I use the terms primary and nonprimary to differentiate between identities that are core to professional identity versus ones that aren't.

For instance, if being an artist is one of your professional identities, but you only teach art workshops a few times a year, and you make art on commission on the side, then is artist one of your primary professional identities, or is it a secondary or tertiary identity? In this case, it might be a nonprimary professional identity.

A primary professional identity has three key qualities. One, you use it daily, or almost daily. Two, it lights you up and brings you joy. You use it because you absolutely love it, not just because you're good at it. And three, it energizes you. It gives you energy instead of draining you.

A nonprimary professional identity is one that isn't core to who you are in your daily work. To use the artist example above, it's not to say that being an artist isn't important to you. It undoubtedly influences aspects of you and your life, but to figure out your hybrid professional identity, it's about looking at the core of who you are in your work, and that's configured by the professional identities you inhabit most often, as in daily. Hybridity is formed by the professional identities you use most of the time, if not every day.

Many professionals haven't fully deciphered their primary professional identities from their laundry list of all their professional identities. When I ask someone, "What are your core or primary professional identities?" and then they tell me a list of ten things they do, I know that they don't know what I'm talking about. They haven't done this reflective exercise to get clear on their primary versus nonprimary identities.

As discussed earlier, a person can only juggle a few identities at the same time. Somewhere between two to four identities is the approximate cap for primary professional identities. The reason for this is best answered with Venn diagrams and math (Figure 6). If you have two professional identities, let's call them A and B, and you draw a Venn diagram and place A and B in each circle, there's one overlapping space, and it becomes AB. Hence, two professional identities create one hybrid combination. Now, if you have three professional identities, let's call them A, B, and C, and you create another Venn diagram, then this time, there are four overlapping spaces and you get identities AB, AC, BC, and ABC. Three professional identities create four possible hybrid combinations.

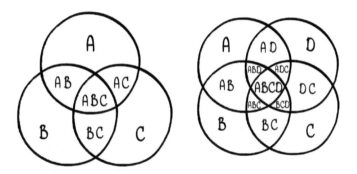

Figure 6. Possible combinations of hybrid identities.

Finally, if you have four professional identities and you draw another Venn diagram with four circles, the number of overlaps jumps to nine. There are nine intersections from four circles. You can imagine if we scaled this to five or more circles how complex the number of intersections would become. It's exponential.

This also demonstrates that the number of intersections, or hybrid spaces, can be higher than the number of professional identities. Three circles create four intersections, four circles create nine intersections, and so forth. This is also why it's messy and challenging to identify hybridity—there are many possible combinations of professional identities when you map it out.

Looking at the number of possible intersections and hybrid combinations, it isn't viable for a hybrid professional to have more than four primary professional identities. Navigating that many intersections and variations of hybridity is unrealistic unless you're superhuman. This is why I believe two to four primary professional identities is the range for hybrid professionals, with three primary professional identities likely being the sweet spot.

As I said previously, a hybrid professional doesn't have to work from their intersections all the time, nor do they have to work from an intersection if it doesn't feel right or feel like a strength. If the intersection of identity A and identity C isn't your jam, that's fine. Don't use it. Just because it's an option, doesn't mean it has to be used. For me, I probably use my designer/researcher intersection the least, whereas I probably use my artist/educator/researcher identity every day.

A hybrid may prefer to work from certain intersections over others. It doesn't matter. What matters is that they must cross at least two or more identities together and create unique relationships between them to be a hybrid professional.

A person may well have ten or more professional identities, but most of those often fall under the secondary or tertiary levels. They appear only occasionally, and they're not used daily like our primary ones are. Until you know which identities are your primary professional identities, it's challenging to determine what's happening in your intersections, which is fundamental to hybridity.

To figure out your primary professional identities, the best tip is to start by brainstorming all the professional identities you possess. Then narrow it to two or three.

A snapshot of possible professional identities includes:

- Activator
- Connector
- Go getter
- Influencer
- Problem finder

- Instigator
- Navigator
- Cheerleader
- Catalyst
- Visionary

If you go to my website, www.morethanmytitle.com, you'll find a resource section with a free download for a word list that has a bunch of pre-generated professional identities. This tool will jumpstart your brainstorming and help you reconsider what you think your primary professional identities are.

After you feel really good, and I mean very, very certain that you know your two to four primary professional identities, then you're ready to explore the intersections and figure out what you're doing when you're working from them. This is what Chapter 7 covers in depth. Getting clear about your primary professional identities is the first big challenge, and the second is examining your intersections and noticing how to cross over.

KEY IDEAS ABOUT HYBRID PROFESSIONALS

- Know that the biggest struggles for emerging hybrids are getting clear on their primary professional identities and learning how to cross over.

- Appreciate that fully developed hybrids are effortlessly and easily able to cross between their professional identities and work at the intersections at will.

- Acknowledge how the development of consciousness is connected to becoming a hybrid professional. The higher the level of consciousness, the more a professional is able to become the self-author of their identity.

- Note that the number of intersections depends on the number of primary professional identities.

CHAPTER 7

Investigating the Intersections

"I have found a new potential inherent in things—their ability to gradually become something else. This seems to me to be something quite different from a composite object, since there is no break between the two substances."
—**René Magritte, artist**

I'VE MENTIONED THE WORD *intersection* many times because it's a key concept of hybrid professional identity. Before explaining what happens at the intersections, I want to make sure you have a crystal clear understanding of what they are. In this chapter, I'll discuss the concept of intersectionality, then shift into the five core aspects and the inner and outer qualities experienced at the intersections. By studying how professional identities overlap, you can use intersections as a space for (re)thinking and (re)defining your entire professional identity.

The next chapter contains stories of how four hybrid professionals work at the intersections of their multiple identities so you can see some real-life examples. Honestly, the hardest part of this research has been to characterize intersections. Listing qualities of intersections is helpful from a research point of view, but it probably won't help you wrap your head around what happens in them. Sharing stories of real professionals is not only fascinating and entertaining, but it will help you better understand the concept of working at the intersections.

What Are Intersections?

Hybrid professionals result from a combination of identities coming together. In academic literature, we call this *intersectionality*. Applying intersectionality to the study of professional identity opens up new questions and new ways of thinking about professional identity, and it's a critical lens for examining hybrids.

It's fairly easy to understand the word *intersection*. Intersections are where two perpendicular streets meet. We drive through them every day on the way to work. When professional identities intersect, powerful new hybrid identities emerge.

I think of hybridity like ocean waves or chewing gum. When waves crash together in the ocean, water from two waves merges to create one larger wave. If you chew one piece of gum and add another piece of gum to it, the result isn't two pieces of gum, but one larger piece of gum. In both cases, one plus one equals one. The same thing happens when professional identities intersect. The result is one professional identity enriched by parts of the others fusing together. One identity plus another identity equals a hybrid identity. This is why hybridity differs from multiplicity.

Intersections in professional identity have three main attributes:

- Two or more professional identities coexist simultaneously.
- Separate professional identities integrate.
- The sum of the professional identities equals one hybrid professional identity.

Intersectionality is a place where deep knowing, making, and doing occur. Intersections become spaces of translation and transformation, as well as spaces of hybrid professional practices. Thinking about identity in terms of intersectionality can be complicated, messy, and ambiguous. But intersectionality provides a construct to help us see and understand the whole person and how they are shaped by their various identities. Singular identities make up our full identity and inform and affect one another, creating reciprocal structures. A parent brings part of their parent identity into the workplace, but they also bring part of their work identity home.

Laurie Nsiah-Jefferson, director of the Center for Women in Politics and Public Policy at the University of Massachusetts, Boston, describes intersectionality as similar to cooking or baking since we take different ingredients and blend them together to make a whole. I keep emphasizing this point, but it's important: the ingredients make the whole. Two workers may look the same, have the same professional training, and even have the same primary professional identities, but no two hybrids are the same. Hybridity is a professional's unique combination of attributes.

Academic Framing of Intersectionality

Shifting gears, I'll describe the academic background of intersectionality, then bring us back to professional identity. The concept of intersectionality was born out of race, class, and gender studies—cornerstones of human identity across society. Many disciplines apply the concept to their work because it has wide application.

When I learned the term, it made me consider what intersectionality within professional identity would look like and if that was possible. Thus, the idea for this book was born. I've found it a useful construct in explaining the presence and qualities of intersections. Although I focus it solely within the vein of professional identity, intersectionality can be the intersection of any types of identities.

In her article "The Complexity of Intersectionality," Leslie McCall argues that as new trends come into vogue, older fields fall further behind because they're not keeping up with newer thinking, frameworks, and models. She states that interdisciplinary studies sought to remedy these divides, as does the field of intersectionality. She proposed an intercategorical approach to observing relationships as the center of analysis, not an afterthought. The relationships between our identities is what matters in understanding who we are, and that's why intersectionality is such a major theory to connect with the field of professional identity.

Intersectionality references the unique ways we combine different aspects of our identity. A person may be Christian, Canadian, gay, female, millennial, bipartisan, and a host of other types of identities. Identity comprises factors such as ethnicity, sexual orientation, socioeconomic status, religion, age, education, ability, and others. Nsiah-Jefferson says, "Human lives cannot be explained by taking into account single categories, such as gender, race, and socioeconomic status. People's lives are multidimensional and complex." That's why we can't examine humans based on single factors.

Kimberlé Williams Crenshaw, a law professor at Columbia University and executive director of the African American Policy Forum, is credited with coining the term intersectionality in the 1980s. Her intent was to combat privilege and oppression across social discourses because multiple systems of discrimination are at play across laws and policies. Crenshaw elevated intersectionality in a court of law to show how multidimensionality was a more accurate way to examine a person's situation.

For instance, let's consider that a black woman of poverty is on trial. She represents three assigned identity categories, so we should recognize her across all three to describe her social position. But in our judicial system, the court may focus on one identity category over another to make an argument, which unfairly represents the person. This is why intersectionality became important in legal studies, because it reshapes arguments to acknowledge the greater complexities of a person's background. The spectrum of identity and social constructs has to be taken into account to be aware of privilege and oppression that's at play, otherwise we encounter bias and stereotypes.

Journeying into the Intersections

Unexpected things happen when professional identities collide. Tensions, contradictions, and even crises can arise, but so can bold new connections. No two identities blend in the same way. And, as I've explained previously, no two hybrid professionals are the same.

If you're a hybrid professional, do you know what happens in your own intersections? Can you explain it to others? From the interviews I've conducted, most hybrids don't know how to discuss their intersections. Even fully developed hybrids can't easily answer questions about this when I ask them. It takes prodding to help them become enlightened about their own intersections.

I didn't understand my own intersections at first. Only through research and self-reflection did I slowly uncover patterns of what happens in them. Once I saw patterns in other hybrid professionals, I wanted to make these traits apparent to all professionals because what happens at the intersections is critical to guiding a hybrid's ability to talk about their hybridity.

Five Traits of What Happens at the Intersections

In the intersections, hybrids perform in ways that look, sound, and feel different from other workers, especially those considered their peers. Sometimes these differences are small; other times they're distinct and drastic. Either way, there are five traits that commonly occur at the intersections of professional identities, and at least one of these traits is always apparent:

Juxtaposition signifies incongruity and mismatch. When two or more professional identities come together, contrast often results. One professional told me, "I feel like being an artist and being a teacher are almost two opposite things. One is a solitary endeavor and one is craziness in the classroom. I have to navigate the duality between the two." Her professional identities cause her to experience chaos and mellowness at the same time, resulting in contrasting feelings, thoughts, and behaviors in her work.

Condensation is paring down into one. When two or more identities come together, they become one identity. The hybrid is a more concentrated version of all the things they do for work.

Paradoxical relationships signify contradictions or inconsistencies that appear both true and false. An example of a paradoxical statement is "less is more." How can something be both less and more at the same time? That's the paradox. A scientist who's also an artist may sound like a paradox.

Metamorphosis is about transformation, one thing becoming something entirely different. In the intersections, multiple identities metamorphose from separate, unrelated, and independent into an altogether new one.

Crossovers happen when a hybrid moves between two or more professional identities, consciously or subconsciously. This is a type of bridge-building or gateway opening between separate professional identities. Sometimes, a professional finds these doorways and bridges easily, and other times a professional needs guidance, permission, and practice to discover how to allow the interchange between identities to happen.

You might be wondering what these traits look like in context. Let's say a hybrid professional named Sam is part of a marketing team. His four primary professional identities include marketer, game designer, community builder, and performance artist. One day, there's a team meeting to brainstorm a campaign for a new product. Sam throws out ideas like creating pop-up art installations in community playgrounds, hiring a DJ and hosting a neon-themed dance party, or traveling to a corn maze and doing a contest with a live webstream.

To the rest of the team, these ideas feel absurd, or at least a bit farfetched. They're thinking along the lines of developing a new website landing page and buying online ads. But Sam's thinking makes the team laugh out loud—it breaks the ice. It puts them in a different headspace, and a new energy fills the room. New possibilities are entertained. They toss around more ideas, some edgy and wild, some serious and conventional.

For Sam, he's in his zone. He's drawing on his multi-faceted background and identities. While his ideas sound random to some on the team, they're not random to him. He's sharing informed ideas based on combinations of things he's experienced, and he believes these could work well for the current project. It's obvious that his suggestions are highly creative and boundary-pushing. He feels alive and energized in the meeting, able to anticipate pushback from others while his creativity flows.

If you were a fly on the wall, watching Sam in the meeting, and you didn't know he was a hybrid, you'd probably think nothing more of him. But you could tell he brings something to the team that you can't quite put your finger on. You would notice nuances in how Sam shares ideas, how he connects divergent thoughts, and how he navigates from one topic to another, drawing unseen connections.

This is how a hybrid professional can look among a group of other nonhybrid professionals. Sam stands out and fits in. His hybridity is almost imperceptible, yet he's working from his intersections. It's noticeable in the way he's thinking about the project and the ideas he's suggesting. They're just different. The team can feel that difference. They also don't quite get where he's coming from. Sam is weaving together ideas from several disciplines. His primary professional identities are mixing and, as a result, what's happening is crossover between his identities.

Sam is demonstrating what happens at the intersections of professional identities. He's juxtaposing marketing with art installations. He's condensing his identities together. He's displaying paradoxical relationships by turning a marketing meeting into a game and being both serious and playful, and he's metamorphizing into a new kind of marketer.

If you're a hybrid professional, how do you see the five traits appearing at the intersections of your professional identities? Are you juxtaposing professional identities? Are you metamorphosing into something else? Are you condensing identities together? If you notice any of these traits, what are you doing when they happen? That's your hybridity in action. Try to notice specific ways you're portraying any of the five traits so you can communicate that value to others.

The Outward and Inward Qualities of What Happens in the Intersections

In addition to the five traits of what happens in the intersections, there are outward and inward qualities. The outward aspects are what the world sees, typically the skills and actions you perform as a hybrid: your brand, work products, work ethic, management style, and leadership style. The inward aspects are what you feel as a hybrid. These may be unconscious or subconscious, but hybrids experience many positive feelings when they're working in their hybridity that are noticeably different from when they're not.

If you're a client or an employer, you can perceive the outward qualities. This is important, because knowing these signs will help you spot hybrid professionals and ask them questions that relate to their hybridity.

If you're a hybrid yourself, you probably won't be surprised by the inward qualities. But you may not have thought about how these inward qualities correspond to your intersectionality. Knowing them will help you better tune into your intersections.

Below, I've listed these outward and inward qualities—the list isn't exhaustive, but it captures many of the predominant qualities:

Outward signs of a hybrid working in their intersections

- Creativity
- Multitasking
- Code-switching
- Job-crafting
- Making random connections
- Pattern recognition, pattern spotting
- Divergent thinking
- High engagement
- High productivity

- Chameleon-ness
- Uniqueness

Inward signs of a hybrid working in their intersections
- High energy
- Aliveness
- Joy
- Flow, being in a zone of genius
- Job satisfaction
- Belonging
- Engagement
- Productivity
- Clear mindedness
- Ability to anticipate/ forecast
- Full integration (being their whole professional self)
- Thriving
- Unity
- Losing track of time

Knowing the five traits and the inward and outward qualities of what happens at the intersections begs the question, how do hybrid professionals find their intersections? This can be a slow process, with trial and error, so be patient with yourself, give it time, and don't forget to have fun and enjoy experimenting with finding your intersections.

Where to Start When Trying to Figure Out What Happens in the Intersections

My friend Jenn Riffle used to introduce herself as a Whole Foods organic chef. Then she ran a property management and housekeeping business for high-end clients. The last time we talked, she was transitioning into a new line of work, and bookkeeping was at the top of her list of possibilities. From the outside, you may think, "Whoa, this person sounds unfocused," or "That's a lot of job-switching." This casts her in the category of multiplicity, a professional who does one thing and then does something different.

What's difficult to perceive is how Jenn's professional identities connect, and more than that, how they integrate. Because Jenn is a longtime friend, and I've had many conversations with her over the years, I know she is a hybrid professional. Each time she morphs into a new role, she integrates her others into it. I see elements of her as a healer and silk artist (professional identities from her early years) woven into her chef identity and property manager work.

So how can we describe what happens at the intersections of professional identities if hybrids themselves can't articulate them? There are ways to do it if you start from the right line of inquiry. Here's an excerpt from my interview with Brad Bickerton. He makes a comment that became a breakthrough insight about hybrid professionals and working in the intersections:

Me: How do you introduce yourself when you're networking?

Brad: (chuckling) Oh, I say I'm a lawyer, a problem solver, a negotiator, an advisor, a mentor, an analyst. I'm many things. I guess that's what makes me unique.

Me: Exactly. All those different identities make you unique. You're probably using them all day long in different ways. Have you ever thought about how you use them together in certain combinations to be successful in your work?

Brad: Sure. I go back and forth between identities all the time. That's why people want to work with me and call me—because they know I'll be able to help them with their problems.

Me: What does it feel like when you're doing that? What would you call yourself when you're moving back and forth between those identities?

Brad: It feels great. I know I can tap into these different skills and experiences I have and use them with the problem at hand, but I don't know what to call being a lawyer and a businessman and a coach all at the same time. It's just something I do. It's something that naturally happens. It's what makes me unique as a professional.

I'll pause here. Did you notice how Brad perked up when he shared how he felt in his work? This was a consistent reaction among hybrids I've interviewed. The biggest lesson I learned in trying to discover what happens at the intersections was to focus first on positive feelings, as those are almost always immediate indicators of when a hybrid is working from their intersections.

Specifically, I learned to ask about moments when a hybrid feels most energized or most alive, or loses track of time in their work. Answers to these questions became the best clues in discovering hybridity. Hybrids may not be aware of how they do what they do, but they're aware of when they feel their best, and their worst, in their work.

Focus on Feelings to Find Your Intersections

> Truly noticing how you feel in your work and getting specific about what you're doing in your intersections is how you tune into what makes you a hybrid.

To develop into full hybridity, do more of what makes you feel good. If you're a hybrid trying to figure out when you're working from your intersections, ask yourself the questions below. These will lead to deeper self-understanding and self-discovery about what makes up your hybridity. If you're unsure how to answer a question, skip it—you don't have to answer them all. The questions are slight variations of each other that target the same idea of honing into the intersections. Some questions work better for different people:

- When do you feel the most energized or alive in your work?

- What are you doing when you feel joy in your work?
- When do you lose track of time in your work?
- When are you in your flow or zone of genius at work?
- What are you doing when you feel you're crushing it at work?

These questions signal being in hybrid spaces because when you're combining more than one primary professional identity together (primary ones being those you enjoy most and use daily), you feel amazing. When you're using your fullest set of skills and talents, it's obvious that working in the intersections would correlate to a sense of well-being at work.

If you're experiencing low or inconsistent feelings of being lit up in your work, then it usually means you haven't figured out how to combine your professional identities. You may feel stuck because you're not able to use your professional identities together, you choose to or have to compartmentalize your identities by performing them one at a time, there's a sense of rigidity in your work instead of fluidity, or you feel lost or isolated in your career trajectory because your hybrid talents aren't being used in tandem. When primary professional identities intersect, and you know how to work from your intersections, these problems disappear. This is the cross over; some hybrid professionals know how to do this, while others have to learn it.

Crossing Over and Working from the Intersections

The moment when a hybrid attempts to connect their identities is what I call the *crossover*. I mentioned this as one of the five traits, but I'll explain more about how it works. A struggle for emerging hybrids is figuring out how to work at the intersections of those identities. This means they have to learn how to cross over. It's an important element of working at the intersections.

For emerging hybrids, this requires awareness of their primary professional identities, and then practicing at work to get familiar with how to cross between identities. Fully developed hybrids cross over at will, without even thinking about it. Crossing over is something that is continually practiced and developed as a professional's hybridity evolves.

Crossing between identities is one thing to learn, but once you know how to cross over, then it's about learning how to stay in the intersections for longer periods of time. That's another part of the process. Hybrids may move in and out of their hybridity, and that's alright. It may not always be appropriate to be a hybrid. But if a hybrid only experiences their intersections for fleeting moments, then they haven't yet learned how to control or master their hybridity.

It takes a bit of trial and error to discern what your intersections look and feel like and what combination of special work skills you're performing when you're in an intersection. This process requires reflection, self-observation, self-study, and self-exploration, with a lot of curiosity. For instance, if you're a marketing executive, but you also do leadership coaching, and you volunteer as a site lead at a food bank, how might these different professional identities connect? What do they have to do with one another? How do they fit together? How do you see elements of one identity influencing another?

My trick for this is to draw—you guessed it—a Venn diagram. Label each circle with one of your primary professional identities. Let's say your primary professional identities are coder, musician, and guide. Label each circle with one of those identity words, and then contemplate this question, "Who am I and what am I doing when I'm combining my coder identity with my musician identity? Or, my musician identity with my guide identity?" and so forth. I call this professional identity math because you're adding your identities together. This is a great tool to help you visualize and reflect on the intersections, instead of the individual identities, that form your hybridity.

As much as possible, try to disassociate from and forget the actual identity words you labeled in each circle of the Venn diagram. The actions you do, the things you literally say and do in your work, are more important than the job title you give it. Letting go of occupations and identity labels you frequently use lets you investigate who you really are and what you're really doing when you're crossing professional identities. Reflect on the five traits to examine how you're using juxtaposition, condensation, metamorphosis, paradoxical relationships, and crossovers at your intersections.

This activity can feel like a difficult brainstorm. Start with the easiest intersections first. The goal is to see a list of hybrid actions that you do. Afterward, you can reflect on this list and envision a new hybrid title that encapsulates the qualities you brainstormed.

Crossing disparate professional identities isn't something people do fluently. When I look at my intersections, some actions I notice between my identities are creating visual aids and diagrams to make sense of data, and using role plays during meetings to convey new points of view. Being really specific around the actions that happen at the intersections is important. Otherwise, your actions end up sounding generic and that means your hybridity will too.

Here are some guidelines to help you discover when you're crossing over and working at your intersections:

- Get clear on your primary professional identities.
- Focus on how you feel: when you light up the most, and feel joyful or energized. Notice which workstreams make you feel awesome compared to the ones that don't. That's critical information. You can even chart this like an energy bar graph.
- Pay attention to specific things in your work that only you (or very few others) can do. That's an intersection. If you have no clue, then pretend I'm a fly on the wall observing you daily. What exactly would I see you doing? What would I hear you say to clients, colleagues, and coworkers? Note those things.

- Ask your friends and colleagues to point out your unique working style and professional attributes. They provide excellent mirrors of reflection.
- Notice when you're in flow. This is signaled by losing track of time, feeling super energized, or motivated in your work.
- Make a Venn diagram, placing one primary professional identity in each circle, and visually examine the intersections. Write down the things you specifically do in the intersections of two or more professional identities.
- Find jobs or roles that let you be in your intersections as much as possible or all the time. If a role forces you to stay in singularity or multiplicity, you won't be allowed to be in your intersections or reach your hybridity.

If figuring out your intersections feels too tiresome, frustrating, or tricky, then you're likely trying too hard. Stay curious and have an open mind during this exercise. Working from the intersections is when work feels easy, fluid, and fun. You also feel more engaged and produce more value when you're in them. Signs that you're not working at your intersections are when you feel stuck, rigid, lost, or isolated in your work. If you're unclear about what you're doing at the intersections, that's a sign that either you're not a hybrid or you need to do more self-reflection and self-study. It's also a good idea to invite others into this process and ask for their observations of you.

This process is hard to complete in one sitting, so be ready to spend time with this over a few days or weeks. For some people, this identity work is speedy, and for others, they need to let it percolate. The instructional guide at the end of this book has more tools to help you with these steps.

Intersections Are Your Superpowers

Knowing the traits, qualities, and characteristics of your intersections doesn't explain why they matter, yet the intersections unlock everything. In the intersections are where your greatest gifts and talents reside. They're the bright spots that shape your professional identity and set you apart.

It's essential to reflect on how you see the five traits showing up in your own intersections so you can articulate the value of your hybridity. When you're in the job market, developing your professional brand, seeking a promotion, or searching for your next professional opportunity, you need to convey what makes you unique.

If you can't express the value of your hybridity or how you're dissimilar from peers who use hyphens, slashes, and multiple job titles on their business cards, then you'll look like and sound like everyone else with multiple professional identities. Crafting a hybrid job title or being clear about the connections between multiple identities are tools to communicate why hybridity is your competitive advantage.

Maybe you've been asked the question, "What are your superpowers?" Your response reveals what you believe you're exceptional at, the things you can do that no one else can do or do as well as you. Intersections are the source of professional superpowers and why hybrids stand out from the crowd. If investigating your intersections feels hard, then try asking yourself how well you know your superpowers. Can you rattle them off? If you know them, do they sound super, or do they sound average?

Figuring out what you do in your intersections is key to answering the superpower question. Years ago, when I was first asked about my superpowers, I froze. I thought to myself, "Do I have professional superpowers? What are they? What do they look like?" I stumbled to find an answer. I responded with, "My superpowers are solving problems and getting stuff done." The people around me smiled and nodded politely. Then one person chimed in, "Oh yeah? Me too!" If you're trying to express your superpowers as the things that make you unique, then the last thing you want to hear is that someone else is good at that as well.

I realized I didn't know my superpowers. I didn't have an answer because I'd never reflected on them. Moreover, I didn't know how to determine what my superpowers were, aside from randomly brainstorming a list of things I thought sounded cool. To find my true superpowers, I needed guideposts to help me pinpoint where to look, instead of feeling like I was wandering around a forest without a map trying to find a buried treasure. I needed cues to support my self-understanding.

When I deeply reflected on what happens at the intersections of my professional identities, and the times I feel the most energized, joyful, or alive in my work, my superpower list started to form. I wrote:

- I ask questions that haven't occurred to stakeholders and reveal gaps in innovation strategy.
- I make the invisible visible by collecting data sets that don't exist and sharing them in effective visual graphics.
- I listen for the word "no" in all its forms, and push into it to understand blocks.

Today, when I'm asked the superpower question, I say I question the unquestioned to build stronger connections in complex ecosystems. Not only is that more accurate, but it's also tied to my primary professional identities and how they actually intersect. That feels a lot different than saying I solve problems and get stuff done. When I'm juxtaposing, metamorphosing, and crossing over between my identities, I become an inquiry machine. I never realized that about myself before. Nobody had pointed that out to me. I had to take the time to deeply reflect and explore my intersections on my own, and it revealed new insights about myself. This was how I discovered my hybridity.

KEY IDEAS ABOUT HYBRID PROFESSIONALS

- Ask yourself when you feel your best at work. Many hybrid professionals can't directly answer what happens at their intersections without practice and time to reflect, but they can tell you when they feel their most energized and alive in their work.

- Reflect on the traits of juxtaposition, condensation, paradoxical relationships, metamorphosis, and crossing over. Notice if any of these apply to you. If they do, what are you doing?

- Let go of previous labels and job titles you've given yourself. When you remove labels, you start to see who you really are at the intersections.

- Figure out what you do at the intersection of your professional identities, and you'll find your superpowers.

- Remember, intersections matter because they are what makes you stand out as a hybrid. They're what makes you exceptional.

CHAPTER 8

Stories from the Intersections

"A paradox is not a conflict within reality. It is a conflict between reality and your feeling of what reality 'ought to be.'"

—Richard Feynman

KNOWING THAT JUXTAPOSITION, CONDENSATION, paradoxical relationships, metamorphosis, and crossover are five aspects that occur at the intersections of identities is hard to comprehend. We need examples to see what this means. What do the intersections look like in the form of hybrid work?

Following are four stories of hybrid professionals I've interviewed, observed, and followed through the years. I wrote these as short case studies to help you compare and contrast the professional lives of different hybrids. This will illuminate the nuances of hybridity and show what it looks like when people integrate their professional identities together in unimagined and novel ways.

Look for details, actions, and terminology that appear in more than one story. For instance, notice tension between identities that seem to be a mismatch. Is that a juxtaposition because there's so much contrast? Maybe you notice shapeshifting in someone's work experience. Does that seem like metamorphosis? Patterns will become more apparent as you read each story.

TIFFANY JOSEPHS

Creator, Magic Carpet Life

Primary professional identities:
illuminator and accelerator

When Tiffany taps into her hybrid professional identity, she's in her space of absolute genius. Tiffany is founder and CEO of Magic Carpet Life. As her professional identity continues to evolve, she keeps iterating on her business model.

When I met Tiffany a few years ago, she was focused on personal coaching, but now she has transformed her business into a grander vision of offering life-design services. Tiffany creates one-of-a-kind experiences for clients that are inspired by her intuition. She thinks of herself as an activator and energy channel.

One time, when she was in Santa Barbara leading a retreat, Tiffany decided the group would do a scavenger hunt in the historic home where the retreat was taking place. The house overlooked the ocean, whales surfaced in its waters each morning, and rose gardens surrounded the premises. It was an idyllic setting. Tiffany had brought special objects with her such as a genie lamp, a glass slipper, and other eccentricities to allow participants to get in touch with their own inner stories.

One morning during the retreat, while participants were meditating and taking in the sunrise, Tiffany hid the objects around the house, tucking notes inside them or adding other surprise touches. When participants returned, they had 20 minutes to scour the house and find the objects. Each person carried a velvet pouch in which to place what they found. The aim of the activity was to trust that the universe was steering them toward clues and that each object found by a participant was meant for them to find. When the time was up, Tiffany guided them to look at what they collected, asking each person to explain why those objects spoke to them in a certain way. "I remember the unfolding of that. It created a space for magic to happen. I invited other magicians to come in and give meaning to something and made it be this really powerful, fun, experience. It was a magic carpet ride to help them hear transmissions from their soul."

Even though the scavenger hunt example probably sounds whimsical, and might be better suited for a group of six-year-olds, if you ever meet Tiffany, you'd see that she's an astute businesswoman. Magic Carpet Life is a successful business for adults. Tiffany's primary professional identities, are being an illuminator and accelerator. When she combines those identities together, she produces extraordinary experiences, and she transports people on what she calls, magic carpet rides.

What happens when Tiffany's professional identities merge is pure magic. She takes ordinary things, like a scavenger hunt, and adds her own twist. Tiffany's methods of coaching and leading retreats are unlike other professionals who say they also lead retreats and do coaching. The scavenger hunt was one example, but there are countless other ways in how Tiffany works and operates her business that are full of her hybridity.

In her intersections, Tiffany metamorphosizes into a professional who, in her words, "creates awakening experiences that lead people to their magic." She transcends her old, professional job titles and labels. Now, she's an accelerator and illuminator of all kinds by blending her coach, orchestrator, thespian, and influencer professional identities together.

JUSTIN GITLIN

Principal of Cacheflowe

Primary professional identities:
creative, developer, musician

As a co-founder of Ello, Mode Set, and Oh Heck Yeah, among other organizations, and with clients like Nike, Google, Dell, Coca-Cola, Capital One, the North Face, and the Denver Art Museum, Justin has his fingers in all kinds of things. He calls himself a creative developer, but what he does is build video games, interactive installations, websites, and mobile apps. In his professional bio, he describes the way he works as moving between parallel worlds of software development, music, and multimedia production, which is evident in all the projects he creates. Likewise, as a musician, he performs as Cacheflowe and even in that, he calls himself a genre-crossing musician. He is not only a boundary crosser of disciplines, but also a boundary crosser of sounds.

If you asked one of Justin's clients to describe him, some would say he's their chief technology officer, others would say he's their technical executer, and others would say he's a magician. Justin's clients don't know how he does what he does, which is why his clients are blown away that what he can do is even possible. Justin's objective is to take a cool idea and turn it into a reality from the technical side. Few people can do what he does.

When Nike, Jordan, and Footlocker teamed up to open an exclusive pop-up retail experience called Sneakeasy on Wall Street in New York City, they hired Justin to build out the digital components. The goal of the shop was to riff off of a traditional speakeasy, where what's inside is a surprise, and provide sneaker fans with surprise drops, the term for new releases in sneaker culture. Shoes are displayed in a setting that looks like a futuristic bank vault, and dispensed through a door that looks like a safe deposit box.

While Justin didn't work on the physical concept, he made all the technology work, including twenty different screens with synced animations, an iPad inventory system for the customer experience, an LED ticker screen to alert customers of inventory changes, and a cross-fading soundtrack between audio loops that was timed to the opening of the Boing box, another experiential component. Between the company partnerships, the store concept, and the types of physical and digital technology involved to make this happen, Sneakeasy represents a hybrid shopping experience from the consumer's point of view, while Justin demonstrates his hybrid professional identity by crossing over, condensing, and juxtaposing countless traditional elements together.

Dancelab is another incredible example in Justin's portfolio. Dancelab was an installation he did for the Denver Art Museum in collaboration with Wonderbound, a dance company, and Legwork, another design group. Inside Dancelab, a dark gallery space, wall projections directed visitors to follow specific dance moves choreographed for the exhibit. As visitors did different poses, a camera captured their movements and stitched them together to make a large-format, MTV-like dance video that was projected alongside animated graphics. This interactive experience got people moving and made them part of the installation in a way no other museum has ever done.

The exhibit was more than a creative project that defied traditional art, it became a community-building activity that made dance moves more accessible and lowered people's self-consciousness about dancing in public. To say Justin is a creative developer is like saying the Grand Canyon is a river, or the Taj Mahal a tomb.

AMY REICHLIN

Director of Leadership Development and Training
Primary professional identities:
artist, hostess, strategist, facilitator, coach

There's party planning Amy, coach Amy, corporate Amy, decorating Amy, and branding Amy. That's how Amy Reichlin described herself to me during our interview.

"How would you encapsulate that into one professional identity?" I asked her.

"Well, one parent used to call me the 'Magical Elf' because I could wear so many hats, and I would show up with bells on whether I was giving a presentation to parents or repainting the hallways," she replied.

Today on LinkedIn, Amy's describes herself as director of leadership development and training of her own firm, Amy Reichlin Consulting. This is the title Amy gave herself. Yet, Amy often gets pushback to call herself an executive coach, which actually appears in the header of her LinkedIn profile. What Amy says she does is develop leaders;

whether her client is a stay-at-home mom or a CEO, she believes everyone is the leader of his/her/their own life. Her passion and gift is to see the seed of her client's selfhood that perhaps has been buried, and to create the conditions for it to emerge, be celebrated, and manifest into the best, most authentic version of the diverse leaders she works with.

When I spoke with Amy a couple years ago, she was on a precipice. She was worried about what other people thought her title should be. "What is it that I do? And, what do I want to call it?" she pondered aloud. She was in a real moment of finding her hybrid professional identity.

"When I'm in public, my preference is to say I'm an executive coach and a facilitator, and if I have enough time, I explain I combine my inherent creativity with my deep knowledge of content to create multisensory experiences where people have a good time but also learn and remember concepts."

Like many hybrids, Amy was torn between using familiar language that quickly connects with her audience, while at the same time, she knew it wasn't enough to express who she really was. Amy danced between how to make her highly unique skill set make sense for other people, while at the same time, knowing she's so much more than just an executive coach or a facilitator.

As is the case of many hybrids, Amy's journey to her current career is fascinating, nonlinear, and full of juxtapositions and unexpected components. The short story is that after college, Amy designed shoes for Sam & Libby. Then she went into nonprofits and later an educational software company, before enrolling in business school in an attempt to find where she fit in the work world.

This is when Amy's confidence plummeted. She became depressed, partially because she had to put away her creative side to be more analytical, but also because she was faced with difficult life issues. She felt alone. In therapy, Amy took a liking to psychology, something she had never studied.

It wasn't until after business school and working at various dotcoms that Amy truly hit a wall and decided to go on a whole different career path. She enrolled in another degree program, this time to study psychology at Naropa University, an institution known as a leader in contemplative education and Buddhist-inspired studies. For a period of time, Amy worked with people who had mood disorders.

Despite this career change, Amy still didn't feel fulfilled, so she did a stint in market research and branding. However, this didn't meet her professional needs either. She wanted to connect more deeply with people. Finally, Amy got a certificate in coaching, and that's when she felt her professional identity click into place. Bouncing from one career to another may seem like indecisiveness or lack of focus, but for Amy, she was unearthing her hybridity. Each role brought her closer to discovering that she didn't have to choose, she could blend all of her identities into one. It also gave her exposure to a wide array of contexts, allowing her to have true empathy for people from a large range of backgrounds and professions. This serves her well on a daily basis.

In her early forties, Amy reinvented herself and built the professional identity she had been searching for. "This is when I emerged," Amy told me about this period of her life. "I created my brand of coaching, which was life coaching at first. I had a prize box, like at the dentist, with cute little things in it to give clients." Amy lit up fondly as she recalled this memory. I could sense this was when she realized she could combine her multiple identities and be the kind of professional she had been yearning to be.

From here, Amy journeyed into her full hybridity. She was asked to work at MacIntosh Academy, a private K–8 school, during a major leadership transition when the school was in crisis. Over the course of a few months, she transformed the school from the inside out. The first thing on her agenda was to restore a sense of safety and optimism to a system that had been deeply traumatized by previous leaders. She created opportunities for teachers and parents to name their frustrations and be validated. She created systems that restored order to a chaotic operating system. She applied her leadership development strategies and transformed the atmosphere and culture of the school from downtrodden to energized, thriving, and vibrant. She brought lasting change by utilizing all of her professional identities in concert in a way she had never been able to before. It was an immensely gratifying experience for her.

Afterward, Amy's hybridity took off. With a renewed sense of herself, Amy relaunched her coaching business. Instead of offering typical leadership development services,

Amy offered learning events with titles like "Buddha + Booze" or "Emotions + Potions." The names alone give a slight glimpse into what they involve.

In her training and team building exercises, Amy weaves together mindfulness, playfulness, business skills, leadership development, neuroscience, and emotional intelligence—talents derived from her primary professional identities. Instead of leading teams through half-day workshops with banal slide decks, Amy mixes cocktails to match each lesson. The unique sensory experience and novelty of each cocktail helps the brain get curious and retain key concepts she teaches.

Everything Amy uses in her facilitation is deliberate and intentional for learning purposes yet highly creative and original. She plays music and plugs disco lights into meeting room walls. She brings miniature snow globes and flashcards with spinners to teach about emotional intelligence and how to have difficult conversations. As an attendee at one of Amy's learning events, I was impressed by the amount of rich, science-based content she packed in alongside a diversity of tactile and interactive activities. Amy was constantly working at the intersections of her professional identities. Psychology, design, and leadership strategy were highly intertwined.

Finding the balance between living and embodying her brand is the challenge Amy continues to grapple with. She wants her brand to feel smart, playful, elegant, and creative while also embracing her legitimate business background with an MBA from Kellogg. Amy isn't trying to be playful and fun to be showy—she does it because it's part of how she lives her professional identity.

As a hybrid professional, Amy wants her work to be seen as relevant so clients want to hire her, but her real desire is to work with people on a soul level. Amy shared with me, "I want to bring people home to themselves." That's what happens when Amy works in her intersections. There is no job title for that unless Amy gives it a title.

FRED STUDER

Chief Marketing Officer, TIBCO

Primary professional identities:
storyteller, experience designer, engagement officer

Fred Studer started his career in finance as an accountant. Then, he got into software, which led to working for large software giants, and eventually, he became a chief marketing officer, which is where he's now positioned within major tech companies. Because of his diverse professional background, he speaks the language of different departments—aka code-switches—but even he is surprised that he's ended up as the chief of marketing. It's not a position he ever imagined moving into. Nevertheless, Fred thrives in it.

From the exterior, you wouldn't know Fred is a hybrid professional because he has a big corporate role. Within moments of starting the interview, I asked him to tell me about how he works. He revealed this about how he runs a meeting:

> I like to draw a design of everything we're going to do. Anytime I go to a whiteboard people go, "Uh, oh, we better start recording Fred." Essentially, I like to draw a design of how we want our customers to experience everything.
>
> Last week we were designing a new email campaign. Although that might seem simple, my team says, "Great, we're going to write an email, and then we're going to send it to a bunch of people." And I say, "Guys, we have to think about where they are on a cycle. It's a buyer's journey, and we can't send the same email to a person. We have to orchestrate this in more of a strategy. It's not just one email, it's a couple, and if they click, where do they go? If it's a website, what does that website look like? If another team calls them, how do they know the email went out?"
>
> Mostly, my team sits and looks at me when I do this. They all get it. Then, they start connecting the dots. I also tell them we could also be wrong. Why don't we do some testing? Let's write some of this and see if it resonates with real customers. We'll do this once a week, designing experiences for our sellers and our customers.

It's clear that Fred has a strong command of marketing and how to build strategy, so I ask him more questions to understand his intersections. How is he crossing and combining his skills and expertise together? What does that look like in his work? He responds by telling me:

I don't notice [how I work] until somebody brings it up. I get so passionate when I'm working. My team has seen this happen numerous times, especially the ones closest to me. When there's a new person on the team, they start to ask questions because they haven't witnessed that space when I'm in that motion. More senior members of my team will say, "Everyone, just pause, right now Fred is in the flow, and all of this will make sense in about five minutes. Studer gets in this thing, and you're not going to believe what happens."

I forget that I get like this until that moment happens, and I think to myself, "I've got to try to show people what this crazy mind of mine is doing, and help them see it so that maybe they might be able to do something like that too."

I've been in this product area for so long. I know these audiences, and now I know enough to be dangerous about technology. I literally get into a zone, and it's kind of like that Will Ferrell moment when he's debating the Ragin' Cajun, and he goes through this whole 60 seconds of economic policy. I tell myself, "I don't even know where that came from." So sometimes, even I don't know how I do it.

The part that perked my ears was when Fred told me his team sees when he's in flow, and they tell each other to wait. Even Fred commented that he gets into a zone because he knows the product area and audiences so well that he can see how everything fits together and what needs to happen—the systems of systems consciousness that Kegan theorized in Chapter 6. In the story that Fred told about his work, he is undoubtedly working from his intersections. His team could sense it. He could sense it. It was palpable, and it was indescribable. They all knew what was happening, but no one could explain it.

Last, I love Fred's aside where he reflected how he'd love to explain what's happening in that crazy mind of his so others could do it too. The truth is, that's exactly what hybridity is. It's a force that's bigger than words and unique to each individual. You can't train someone to be the kind of hybrid you are.

Fred, Tiffany, Amy, and Justin are very different types of professionals. From the outset, they might sound like they have multiplicity, but when you read how they work, you realize they're hybrid professionals because of what happens in their intersections. Their hybridity is noticeable in the way they talk and in the way they work. Colleagues and clients of hybrids pick up on their unique work styles, and respond to it with curiosity, enthusiasm, and compliments. They may not see it as hybridity, but they sense the uniqueness of what they're witnessing.

- Reflect on moments in your workday to isolate when you're using your hybridity. When are your professional identities blending together?

- Notice which story resonated with you. Why did it resonate? How does it help you see your hybridity?

- Realize that hybridity can happen in subtle, not obvious acts. Hybrids are usually unconscious of their hybrid methods, and that's why they're hard to articulate.

- Practice using stories to depict your hybridity and help others see what makes you a hybrid.

PART THREE

Preparing for a Future of Hybrid Professionals

Recruiting, Hiring, and Managing Hybrid Professionals

"We don't have rigid job descriptions because they promote rigid thinking and suddenly you think there is a fixed job for you. If you give people flexible pathways, people evolve into lots of roles they would have never thought they were interested in."

—*Sridhar Vembu, founder, Zoho Corporation*

HYBRID PROFESSIONALS ARE MULTIDIMENSIONAL nonconformists who work in unconventional ways. They're not all necessarily rebels, misfits, or rule breakers, but there are fundamental differences that should be considered when employing them. When you hire and manage someone who integrates multiple professional identities, and those identities don't seem like they fit together, you employ someone who will likely also test your existing organizational structures. So, what should recruiters, managers, and leaders know and be able to do to attract, hire, manage, and retain hybrid professionals?

After all, hybrids possess desirable, one-of-a-kind capabilities. They're the type of talent companies clamor for. The question employers should ask themselves isn't whether they should hire a hybrid professional; the question is whether they'll be able to retain them once they're recruited. Hybrid professionals only stay in settings and roles where their full hybridity is valued and can shine all the time.

A changing world means a changing workforce. Leaders claim they want to be innovative to stay ahead of the competition, and they desire employees with unique skill sets to achieve a competitive advantage. But before they can do that, leaders need to see the benefit of hiring hybrid professionals who don't fit neatly into boxes created by human resources or by old paradigms. Not only that, but leaders and managers need to be willing to make necessary accommodations internally to support this type of professional.

Hiring and retaining hybrid professionals means employers need to commit to continually checking on hybrids to understand the nuances of what they need to be successful. This may differ from standard management practices. In other words, it's not enough for an employer to say they're willing to hire a hybrid professional without acknowledging it also requires some level of internal reconfiguration to accommodate a hybrid to do the work they're capable of doing. Hybrid professionals thrive in roles that are flexible, which can impact everything from performance targets to reporting structures.

In simple terms, employers need to do three things. First, employers need to broaden their perspective beyond experts and generalists, and acknowledge the existence of hybrids. Hybrids are more than expert-generalists. A hybrid integrates different professional identities together and is the sum of those identities. That means they possess various depths of expertise along with general knowledge and merge skills into an entirely new set of abilities.

Second, employers need to employ hybrid professionals for their hybridity. A developer is not just a developer anymore, and a salesperson is not just a salesperson anymore. They may also be strategists, innovators, speakers, therapists, airplane pilots, yoga teachers, organic chefs and more. Hybrids work in an interdisciplinary fashion. In fact, the multiple professional identities a hybrid possesses informs and influences the professional identity that attracted employers to them in the first place. Don't disregard a hybrid's other professional identities, realize these are the reasons the hybrid excels at what they do for work.

Third, employers need to learn alongside hybrids and shouldn't expect to ever fully understand a hybrid professional. Hybrids are a new type of worker we have yet to consider in the workforce, and we need to continue studying what they need in the workplace to be successful. It may never be clear to an employer, manager, colleague, or even to the hybrid themselves how they do exactly what they do. Despite my efforts to provide an analysis in this book, hybrid professionals work in ways that will always be difficult to capture in words alone. Watch what they do, appreciate what they do, and ask them what they need to feel supported to do better.

Recruiting, hiring, training, and retaining hybrid professionals requires openness to establishing and implementing processes and protocols that are different from the needs of workers who are non-hybrids. This is because if a hybrid isn't hired for their full hybridity, they'll get bored or frustrated and likely leave the job. Or, if they're hired for their full hybridity but not valued for it once they're hired, they'll feel resentful and deceived.

Recruiting and managing hybrid professionals is a large topic that deserves deeper attention. This chapter provides a basic overview of what an employer or client should do if they want to hire a hybrid professional or if they encounter a hybrid professional during the hiring process. Hybrid professionals shouldn't be treated as or confused with generalists or experts. The reason is those terms misconstrue that a hybrid professional is only one or the other, which minimizes their hybridity.

Hybrid professionals work at the intersections of their professional identities. This is a critical distinction, and it's a concept that's lacking from current recruitment and employment practices and discussions. Not all workers fit the binary of experts or generalists. The future needs to include hybrid professionals alongside other types of professionals.

Why Hire a Hybrid Professional in the First Place?

Hiring a hybrid positively impacts business growth and culture. One value a hybrid brings is they can act as a bridge and translator between otherwise disconnected groups of professionals, perhaps an engineering team and a sales team, since a hybrid's identity might be a combination of those areas. There are documented benefits of hiring cultural misfits, most notably because they bring diverse ideas and perspective, which sparks creativity and innovation in organizations.

Leaders and organizations must be willing to hire hybrid professionals for their hybridity. The fact that a hybrid can't be pigeon-holed for what they do is what differentiates them from other workers. A hybrid's expertise is informed and comprised by their range of professional identities. Hire them for that. Hire a hybrid because they have a unique composition of attributes.

The book *Rebel Talent* was a breakout business book of 2018. It argues that leaders should hire people who are rebels because workers who don't fit the cultural norm, who are seen as unconventional, and who act as boundary pushers are good for business. Author Francesco Gino explained that rebels are changing the world for the better with their unconventional outlooks. Hybrid professionals share a lot in common with rebels.

Gino's concept of rebel talent, and her research of how they work, has a lot of overlap with hybrid professionals. Both rebels and hybrid professionals break rules, or have trouble following them, because they're nonconformists and challenge the status quo. They're also both known to be masters of innovation and reinvention. They come up with ideas no one else sees. Gino concludes rebels offer immense value to companies and that every company needs them if they are to grow and innovate.

The catch is that when a worker is considered an outsider, not belonging to one department, specialty, or field, they struggle to fit in, be respected, or be taken seriously. Hybrid professionals are often misunderstood by colleagues, but trusted peers see that hybrids are amalgams of original thinking and bring unique perspectives to the table.

Rules to Hire Hybrid Professionals

When hiring, managing, or working with a hybrid professional, take these points into consideration. I call them rules, but they're more like strong recommendations:

Hybrids aren't *this* or *that*. They have multiple professional identities. They are generalists and experts. The job of the hiring manager or employer is to figure out to what degree of each they are, and how the hybrid's expertise and general knowledge fits together to support you in executing what you need done.

Don't box hybrids in or pigeonhole them. HR departments don't like hybrids because they stretch management structures and classification systems. My recommendation for employers is: figure it out. I know it's difficult, and it will test you, but this is where hybrids push traditional limitations, even before they're hired. Don't box them into one thing. It will probably cause problems for you and the hybrid professional later.

If an employer is willing to hire a hybrid professional because they see the incredible talent they bring, then that employer will also have to be willing to reconsider certain internal company policies and structures. This might mean a hybrid professional co-reports to two different departments, works across two different teams, or even has two different bosses. Two is just an easy number to type, but it might be a different number. You get the idea.

Hybrid professionals often stretch job descriptions to feel accommodated and valued for what they bring to a role. Employers have to be flexible in what job title they assign them and how the job description is worded. It must somehow represent that the hybrid's hybridity is encouraged. The more a hybrid's hybridity can flourish, the more they will show up as their full professional selves in their work and contribute high value in return.

Don't minimize or cut apart a hybrid's hybridity. An employer can't cherry pick the parts they like or want the most for the role out of the different professional identities a hybrid brings to the table. That's not how it works. An employer has to be willing to hire a hybrid professional for all they bring, the full enchilada.

A hybrid's hybridity shouldn't make an employer nervous, rather they should be curious and excited to see how the hybrid professional's unique identities will bring fresh abilities and insights to the company. For instance, if an employer is enthusiastic about a hybrid professional's background in user research, brand development, and toy making, but doesn't see the value in their beer brewing business, they shouldn't be dissuaded from hiring that hybrid, and they should absolutely encourage the beer brewer identity to show up at work. An employer doesn't have to know how the beer brewing will be fruitful to his company, he has to trust that it will be. Although, this is where the hybrid professional needs to draw a compelling connection for the employer so the value is more transparent, which leads me to rule four.

Understand what makes a hybrid a hybrid. It's the employer's job and the hybrid professional's job to be clear on the different professional identities a hybrid possesses and how those identities fit together. It's not enough for a hybrid to list their primary professional identities for the employer. The important aspect is the intersections. An employer should also understand the significance between the relationships of the professional identities. This is a critical component to communicate.

Hiring Process: For Hybrid Professionals

Finding the position that's the right fit for a hybrid professional can be a daunting task. This is why it's crucial for hybrid professionals to clearly articulate their hybridity to prospective employers. Hybrid professionals should be able to explain what they need to feel valued and fulfilled as a hybrid in the role.

Surrounding yourself by work or finding a workplace that values your hybrid professional talents allows you to cease the whiplash of shifting from one identity to another. No more ping ponging back and forth and feeling disconnected daily. Choosing between being this or that in one job to the next is the old way of working. It doesn't have to be that way for hybrid professionals. It's a matter of getting clear on what makes you a hybrid in the first place so you can declare your identity in a way that makes sense.

As hybrid professionals, we know it's important to showcase our value and help employers recognize we have multiple types of expertise in a range of things. To an outsider who has never met us and has no context of what we do, we often come across as a list of things or a list of titles. We often pose an identity conundrum for employers and clients. What are they supposed to hire us for when they can't make sense of what we do?

Who are you and what do you do are the two questions people are trying to assess and understand about us all day, every day. As hybrid professionals, make it easier on potential employers to understand who you are and what you do. Remember the following:

Know your primary professional identities and keep them consistent. These are the two, three, but no more than four professional identities you possess that you use on a frequent, or daily basis, and that light you up and energize you the most. These shouldn't change from job interview to job interview, but they can evolve over time. If it's been a year or more, you might be due for a refresh. Primary professional identities are the core professional identities you want to use in your work and want to be known for. If you weren't able to use one of your professional identities regularly, you would feel a loss and would become frustrated by limiting the usage of it. Your goal is to experience your professional identities as fully as possible everyday.

Be prepared to explain how your primary professional identities fit together. You will need to articulate the relationships between your professional identities so that they are clear to you as well as to others. What do you do when you weave your professional identities together? Then, also explain why this matters for the role you want. Connect the relationships of your identities back to the job at hand.

Explain that you're a hybrid professional and what that means. It might be helpful to use the term hybrid professional when going through a hiring process. If they haven't heard that term before, be ready to explain it succinctly.

Remember, blending and combining your different professional identities together is why you perform in ways that no one else can perform. Offer a couple of specific examples.

Emphasize how your unique value lies at the intersections of your professional identities. This is what differentiates you. This is why they want to hire you. These are the selling points that make you stand out. This should not be generic language. *Show* instead of telling by providing rich stories and even consider bringing a portfolio that offers pictures of your work so they can see what you've done because of your intersections.

In Chapter 3, I offered several suggestions as to how to introduce yourself if you're a hybrid professional including what to say in person, in an email, and in your cover letter. Go back to this section if you're preparing for a new job.

Hiring Process: For Recruiters and Hiring Managers

Recruiters and hiring managers need to be familiar and comfortable with how to screen hybrid professionals for positions. They should know certain questions to ask and clues to look for that helps them better see the unique value the hybrid brings compared to other candidates. And, once they find the right fit, keeping hybrid professionals in a position for a long period can be tricky as well.

If you want to work with or hire a hybrid professional, there are a few things you should know about them. Hybrid professionals flourish in companies and situations where their hybridity is valued, not minimized or picked apart. If you don't let a hybrid professional use their full hybridity, then they probably won't work for you for very long or they'll stay, but they'll become cranky. You don't want to go through the hassle of hiring a new person, and they don't want to feel trapped in a position that doesn't allow their full hybridity to be utilized.

Hybrid roles should be explicitly called out as such and described as hybrid positions. Start defining open positions as hybrid positions and actively seek hybrid professionals for their hybrid abilities. This will help ease frustration that employers and job seekers experience in terms of expectations.

Top companies like Google, Microsoft, and Deloitte used to hire based on ranking individuals against scales, but then realized that great talent can't be boiled down to numbers. It wasn't working for finding the best talent. They needed other ways of discerning who would really succeed in their companies.

Rankings are based on one-dimensional thinking. Todd Rose, author of *The End of Average*, has a few principles about how to measure humans, and one of them is that individuality is based on jaggedness. This means when trying to assess things that are complex, like creativity or talent, there are multiple dimensions that matter. Mathematically speaking, these dimensions are not strongly linked, there is a weak correlation between each one.

While averagarianism, comparing everyone against the average, was a tool that worked for the industrial workforce, it's holding us back in the modern economy. It compels us to conform to a certain standard that doesn't exist. No one is average, so why are we still measuring people against that?

We can only compare people against themselves and their own improvement or changes in their performance over time. As Rose puts it, "We have lost the dignity of our individuality. Our uniqueness has become a burden, an obstacle, or a regrettable distraction on the road to success." Distinguishing talent is about letting each person show what makes them the best in their own unique way, not comparing them to an average. Rose has dedicated his research to the science of the individual because it's individuality that matters, not average and rank-order. Rose states that in the "human qualities that matter most (like talent, intelligence, personality, and character) individuals cannot be reduced to a single score."

The breakthrough for the companies I mentioned above was they realized there are multiple ways for potential employees to be talented. They just had to discern what type of talent they really needed. As employers, they needed to be more thoughtful and sensitive to multiple dimensions of assessment. Moving past GPAs, test scores, and educational background enabled these companies to focus on different types of information and how they wanted candidates to present it. This lesson is an important one for the modern workforce, which is undergoing shifts from traditional long-term employment to more part-time and independent contract work.

How are you assessing qualifications in your talent pool? Are you ranking and sorting based on scales and quantitative marks that compare candidates against the average? Try again. This will not help you find or recruit hybrid professionals who don't benchmark well on these types of measures. If you're looking for innovators, rebels, risk takers, and people who just plain old think and work differently, then you must reconsider how you're assessing them.

Hiring Tips for Recruiters and Hiring Managers

Look past any job hopping or disconnectedness in a resume. That may be a clue that they're a hybrid, not an unfocused or uncommitted worker. You should still ask about this during interviews, but don't dismiss them based on this point.

Ask for work examples, work products, or rich stories so a hybrid professional can show you what they've done. Don't rely on verbal description. Hybrids do things that defy language. It's much better if you can see or feel what they're capable of. You'll develop a better understanding.

Focus on when a hybrid feels their best at work to learn about what happens in the intersections of a hybrid's professional identities—the heart of what makes them uniquely valuable. Ask them to describe times when they feel their best or most energized in their work and then ask what they're doing in those moments. This is an easier way to dig into the intersections rather than asking direct questions about the intersections.

Hiring Questions for Recruiters and Hiring Managers

Begin by assessing whether a person is a hybrid professional. Here are suggested questions to use:

1. What are your professional identities? What are your primary professional identities—the ones you use the most and that bring you the most joy?
    a. Do you have multiple professional identities? (If it confuses the person, skip and move on.)
        i. If so, what are they?
        ii. Do you use these identities separately, one at a time, or do you feel they work together? If so, please describe how.
2. Are you a hybrid professional? (If it confuses the person, skip and move on.)
    a. If they answer yes: What makes you a hybrid?
    b. How does your hybridity look?
3. When do you feel your best or most energized in your work? What are you doing in those moments? (Focus on feelings to discover when a hybrid is working in their intersections, which is where they're hybridity is formed.) Alternative questions:
    a. What lights you up at work? What are you doing when this happens?

b. What brings you joy in your work? What are you doing when this happens?

c. What energizes you in your work? What are you doing when this happens?

4. How do your different professional identities fit together? Can you explain the relationship between them? (Try to understand the intersections of a hybrid's professional identities). Additional questions:

a. What are your superpowers? How do your professional identities factor into your superpowers?

b. Do you know what happens when you cross your identities together? Explain or provide a story.

c. Do any of the following occur when you cross your professional identities together? If so, elaborate.

i. Metamorphosis: How do you morph from one thing into another between your professional identities?

ii. Juxtaposition: How do your professional identities seem like a mismatch but still work together?

iii. Paradoxical relationships: How do your professional identities contradict each other or have incongruities yet still work together?

iv. Condensation: How do your multiple professional identities form into one?

5. What is the unique value of your hybridity?

Managing Hybrid Professionals in the Workplace

The future requires leaders and companies who reimagine the types of professionals they hire. The future needs leaders and companies who openly recruit hybrid professionals. It's time to acknowledge that hybrid professionals belong in the workplace and are valued for all the professional identities they bring. They shouldn't have to choose one professional identity over another to fit in or get hired. The reason we hire them is for their hybridity.

Hybrids need to have conversations with employers to collaboratively develop new structures that support their hybridity since these don't exist yet. Businesses haven't thought to invent tools, policies, or practices specific to hybrid professionals, until now. Teams, managers, supervisors, and clients should adapt onboarding, training, leadership, and management systems to accommodate hybrid professionals, just like generalists and experts are provided with certain conditions to perform well and thrive in the workplace. This will be an ongoing conversation as society collectively learns and discerns what hybrid professionals need.

Working in the intersections means using approaches that are flexible, open, and embrace all of a professional's identities. In his book *Free Agent Nation*, Daniel Pink describes that work that is "personalized, customized, [and] fashioned to the individual," this is what free agents seek, and I believe this applies to hybrid professionals too. When a hybrid's work feels restricted, they don't perform well because they're stuck in a box instead of using their range of professional identities.

The first step of learning how to hire, manage, and retain hybrid professionals is recognition and awareness of the concept. The next step is to create ways to make hybrid professionals feel a sense of belonging and appreciation for the hybrid value they bring. The ultimate goal is for employers to allow hybrid professionals to show up as their full hybrid identity every day at work and to reward and celebrate them for their hybridity.

Try setting performance goals tailored to hybrid professionals. Ideas include:

- Number of new connections/cross-disciplinary solutions the hybrid contributed over the past year that were adopted or positively influenced the organization in some way. Specifically calling attention to the interdisciplinary nature of the solution as being significant to its success.

- Number of different departments or staff members across an organization the hybrid collaborated with or supported during the year, and examples of the types of transformative contributions the hybrid made to those staff or departments.

- Number of unconventional tools, processes, or work products created by the hybrid that added benefit and demonstrated a blend of unique methodologies. (Especially if these creations went unnoticed because the hybrid may have naturally created them; not as an act of subversion but out of necessity).

- Number of times the hybrid constructively "broke or bent a rule" that positively impacted or shifted the status quo for a team or for the organization, showing their ability to innovate at their intersections.

- Percentage of time the hybrid felt empowered to be their full hybridity and work at their intersections. Also note percentage of time when a hybrid didn't feel empowered to be in their full hybridity and why.

These types of performance goals support how hybrids work, and lets them showcase the power of their hybridity. The contributions hybrids make often add new thinking, innovation, creativity, and improvements to organizations and their products or services.

KEY IDEAS ABOUT HYBRID PROFESSIONALS

- Realize that the emergence of hybrid professionals is reshaping how we recruit, train, manage, and retain talent because hybrids need to be seen and valued for their hybridity.

- Ask hybrids when they feel their best in their work if they can't directly explain their hybridity. Hybrids have to learn how to discuss their hybridity, just as employers and managers need to practice helping hybrids see how they do what they do.

- Continue studying and checking in with hybrids to learn alongside them and find what they need to be their full hybridity.

- Create performance metrics and goals that uniquely reflect the hybridity of a hybrid. It's challenging to decipher how hybrids do what they do, and inter-disciplinarity is a key factor. Be willing to invent new, individualized performance standards.

CHAPTER 10

The Future Is Definitely Hybrid

"Life isn't about finding yourself. Life is about creating yourself."

—*George Bernard Shaw*

THE FUTURE IS BECOMING more hybrid as work becomes more interdisciplinary, interrelated, interwoven, and complex. That means we're also becoming hybrid as we intermix across sectors and work in-between traditional identities and occupations. Today, and into the future, we need to acknowledge a new type of professional: the hybrid.

According to Heather McGowan, a future of work strategist, the what do you do question is irrelevant. She notes that we're moving into an age where people will hold seventeen jobs in their lifetime across five industries. Asking someone what they do won't make sense anymore, because people will change jobs and sectors too often. The norm won't be about what people *do,* but about *how* they work, which shifts the focus to a person's mindsets and identities.

In McGowan's book *The Adaptation Advantage,* she uses an image of an iceberg to describe what's needed for the future of work (Figure 7).

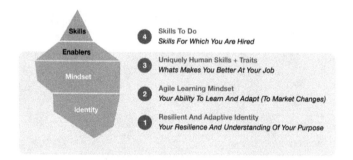

Figure 7. Iceberg image printed with permission from Heather McGowan, Adaptation Advantage: Let Go, Learn Fast, and Thrive in the Future of Work, Wiley, 2020.

She places skills at the top of the iceberg, the part that appears out of the water. This implies skills are what we think are most important and tend to focus on most in education and workforce development. But actually, McGowan argues it's what's beneath the surface that matters more.

At the bottom of her iceberg, deep in the water, is identity. Identity represents our ability to adapt, be resilient, and understand our purpose. She believes this is the first layer in the future of work. After identity comes mindset, which means our ability to learn to adapt as conditions change. The third layer is enablers, which are the unique human traits and skills we possess. Finally at the top, the fourth layer is skills. Essentially, McGowan's iceberg demonstrates that identity is fundamental to the future of work. We have to understand our professional identities and be willing to constantly change.

McGowan also states that asking a child what they want to be when they grow up is a defunct question, since most of the jobs of the future don't yet exist. Instead she recommends asking youth *how* they want to be when they grow up. She theorizes that adaptability and resilience are critical qualities of future workers. Adaptability is a trait of hybrids because they metamorphize, reshape, and rethink their professional identities to mold them into new ones.

Old conceptions of professional identity are holding us back. That's why we need to embrace new mental models of who professionals are. In his book *A Whole New Mind*, Daniel Pink remarks that the future requires not only different kinds of workers, but also different kinds of thinkers. He writes:

> The last few decades have belonged to a certain kind of person with a certain kind of mind. Computer programmers who could crank code, lawyers who could craft contracts, MBAs who could crunch numbers, but the keys to the kingdom are changing hands. The future belongs to a very different kind of person with a very different kind of mind. Creators and empathizers, pattern recognizers and meaning makers. These people...will now reap society's richest rewards.

When we as hybrid professionals work at the intersections of our professional identities, we use the mindsets and skills Pink references: creating, empathizing, pattern recognizing, and meaning making. New mindsets let us see our work differently and form hybrid identities we didn't previously imagine we could have.

The bottom line is that work, as we know it, is dramatically shifting. For years, we've been using the phrase "I wear a lot of hats," which is slang for "I'm a hybrid professional," because we haven't known what else to call ourselves. For workers who integrate identities, it's time to update our vocabulary with this new term.

The world is becoming more competitive, interconnected, automated, and augmented. In his book *Thank You for Being Late*, Thomas Friedman notes that we are in what he calls the age of acceleration, because the pace of globalization, technology, and climate change are increasing faster than at any time in history and changing the five key realms of workplace, politics, geopolitics, ethics, and community.

With the onset of the acceleration age, established sectors are colliding while others are dividing. Digital and physical realms are merging into augmented realities. Gas and electric energy are combining. Geneticists are breeding new types of foods. Hybrid products and solutions are being brought to market all around us. Doctors are using robots to perform routine surgeries. IT professionals and network engineers are morphing into BizDevOps teams (a combination of business, software development, and operations).

So, if the nature of work is changing, why are professional identity frameworks remaining stagnant? Look at the self-assessment and personality tools that dominate the career advice and professional development market. Myers-Briggs, StrengthsFinder, and DiSC are popular career tools because they help us uncover insights about our strengths. But these assessments don't help us clarify an understanding of our identity, which is who we are and how we want to be in the new economy.

A career advisor may help us hone our professional strengths and clarify our purpose at work, but when does a career coach ask about professional identity? That's the missing aspect of career and professional development.

Old career advice focuses on finding "your why," your passion and purpose, and mapping that to a career. The future is about having a portfolio of professional identities and communicating the unique value that lies at the intersections of those identities. Identity is who you are, not what you do.

In a personal note in 2020, Rafael Sarandeses, head of financial services at Talengo, wrote:

We are evolving from "kind" learning environments to "wicked" learning environments in a world of multiple accelerations [cited by Hogart]. Integrating our career capital in combined identities, to me, seems less like an exception and more like an evolutionary need in the professional realm.

The new workforce is about differentiation, individuality, and defining your special talents. In author Nilofer Merchant's definition, onlyness is a person's distinct spot in the world and the source of new ideas. When multiple professional identities exist in one person, unexpected connections occur, and the value they bring to society and to companies can be tremendous.

McGowan believes the future is more about crafting a professional brand than earning credentials because expertise is defined by a worker's professional brand. That's why hybrid professionals must learn how to articulate what happens at the intersections of their identities, because the intersections are their spaces of expertise.

Currently workers lack tools to describe and talk about their shifting professional identities. Finding your hybrid professional identity is about applying the right tools to help you express the value you bring to the workforce.

Hybrid Jobs Are on the Rise

Cross-sector, cross-disciplinary, and blended background jobs are becoming more prevalent. Although only a handful of companies are using the term *hybrid* in job postings, that's changing. You need to be prepared to show your hybridity on resumes, in cover letters, on LinkedIn profiles, on personal or professional websites, and during interviews. Hybridity should become part of your professional brand.

The year 2016 was called the year of the hybrid job by the job posting platform Glassdoor. Susan Brennan, associate provost and executive director of career education at Wellesley College, was quoted as saying, "In the past a student may have thought of marketing or advertising as a creative role. Today business development and big data analytics are marketing roles so the candidate would need to have both creative and analytical skills." While jobs may not appear to be hybrid from the outside, they certainly require hybrid abilities and cross-disciplinary assets to be successful. Hybrid roles, hybrid skills, and hybrid professional identities are emerging onto the professional landscape.

In 2017, HuffPost published an article titled "The Future Is Hybrid," by Anant Agarwal, the CEO of edX, an edtech nonprofit that provides massive open online courses. Agarwal argued that the hybridization of roles is permeating all industries, and that hybrid professionals must possess business and technology expertise including a range of hard and soft skills. He remarked, "This type of blended background is precisely what employers, who are looking to fill positions that require a mix, or hybrid, background—like a mobile marketer or digital product manager—are looking for." It's time to promote this in our networking, interview and hiring processes, talent management strategies, and value propositions.

We're in an era where the global competition for talent is fierce. Low-skilled jobs are disappearing because of machine learning and AI, and hybrid jobs are on the rise. Workers who possess multiple professional identities but who don't blend them together to form unique, hybrid skills are already struggling to stand out from those who do. Workers who possess multiplicity, even though they are multitalented, must compete against workers who understand how to combine skills and knowledge across disciplines.

Conclusion

The concept of hybrid professionals matters to the future workforce because work is changing, which means roles and professional identities are changing. The tension between being hyperspecialized or having a range of abilities is too binary. As David Epstein writes in his book *Range*, "The challenge we all face is how to maintain the benefits of breadth, diverse experience, interdisciplinary thinking, and delayed concentration in a world that increasingly incentivizes, even demands, hyperspecialization." We need another option. Workers need to be able to be hybrids.

Hybrid professionals will continue to grow as a segment of the workforce. They represent all industries and all disciplines. They are freelancers, entrepreneurs, small business owners, independent contractors, people in career transitions, those about to graduate college, and those inside companies with a single job title.

The emergence of hybrids is reshaping how we recruit,

train, manage, and retain talent because hybrid professionals need to be seen and valued for their hybridity, not just their multiplicity. Hybrids don't fit neatly within traditional hierarchies or organizational structures, and that's why it's hard for employers and clients to know what to hire them for or how to best use their skill sets.

The future is not a workforce of fixed occupations, lifetime career holders, or the binary notion of experts or generalists. Neither is it a world where people need to accumulate yet another identity. Hybridization is about integration—weaving together multiple identities—as well as defining how we want to be seen, named, and recognized. It's how we support integration and interconnectedness between professional identities that matters for the future.

My hope is for employers, managers, leaders, and hybrid professionals themselves to learn how to support these unique professionals in the workplace. I also hope other researchers study the presence and effects of hybrid professionals in the workforce. As a result, perhaps more of them will have the courage to share their experiences. This is a moment to learn more about these professionals, to give this group the attention and guidance they deserve.

If we can understand more about how hybrids connect their professional identities, we'll also uncover more about their uniqueness and what they need to succeed. Studying what happens at the intersections of different professional identities requires more analysis because there's more to uncover, and I'm excited to keep investigating it. More evidence will also reveal ideas for specific types of coaching, mentoring, training, and management tools that might benefit hybrids so they can articulate what they do, find where they belong in the workforce, and advocate for what they need to perform at their best.

Talent managers, human resource directors, career coaches, and executive leadership consultants have reached out to me to discuss their questions about hybrid professionals because they see this trend in the workforce. However, they haven't had the right resources to support their hybrid clients who are struggling with many of the topics covered in this book. When hybrids can articulate who they are at the intersections of their professional identities, then their full professional selves can show up to work, and we can realize their full professional value.

KEY IDEAS ABOUT HYBRID PROFESSIONALS

- Keep pace with shifts in the global economy by creating hybrid roles, jobs, and job titles.

- To stand out in a competitive global talent pool, use hybridity as a differentiator and a competitive advantage. Learn how to clearly communicate your hybridity so your unique value is seen and understood.

- Continue studying and learning about hybrid professionals in the workforce. Ask hybrids about who they are and their experiences in their careers to help create an environment where they can perform at their best.

A Free Instructional Guide To Help You Find Your Hybrid Professional Identity

If you want support on how to become a hybrid professional, you can download a copy of my free instructional guide. The guide takes content and advice from this book and puts it into action, as if I were there coaching you. I'll walk you through the five steps of finding your hybrid professional identity using custom activities.

Get the instructional guide at www.morethanmytitle.com/specialgift

Also, if you're like me and you enjoy visual aids to follow along, I've created a hybrid professional identity workbook to assist you. The workbook is filled with templates, word lists, and diagrams to help you examine your hybridity and design your hybrid job title. You can find my accompanying workbook by searching *More Than My Title Workbook* on Amazon.

Acknowledgments

This book is the result of copious amounts of love, support, late night advice, and words of encouragement from so many individuals who have believed in me and this idea for years. They helped me find my voice and express my vision. I'm incredibly thankful for everyone who joined me on this journey, for one step or many, because every step mattered. I'm touched you cared enough to lend me your ear, your time, and your heart.

My dear friend Brenna Vaughn is my rock. During this process, she told me, "Go write pages and pages and pages to change the world." She has been my relentless cheerleader, and I'm forever grateful to her and her family. There was a team who directly helped with the book development, writing, and launch: Melissa Wilson coached me all the way through, Meg Howard developed the beautiful cover, Gretchen Dykstra did a stellar job editing, Kenzie Crow did outreach and launch support, and Tara Gilboa assisted as a sounding board. I loved working with all of you and thank you for the talent you brought.

My early readers provided the most amazing constructive feedback when the manuscript was still raw: Paul Kim, Matt Duncan, Sue McGurkin, Morely McBride, and Lynn Debilzen, thank you for plowing through the unpolished version and seeing the potential within. There were many interviews that didn't end up in the book, and I want to thank everyone who spoke with me. A special thank you to those who let me feature them: Tiffany Josephs, Amy Reichlin, Ti Chang, Justin Gitlin, Brian Corrigan, Joel Davis, Brad Bickerton, Julie Markham, Jenn Riffle, and Fred Studer.

A number of people played an important role, whether hosting brunches to talk about hybrids, testing activities, sharing resources, sending notes of encouragement, or just giving me a high five. I don't think they realize the impact they've had on me, but I want them to know they have: Betsy Berk, Kristina Hesbol, the Vaughn and Linke families, Casey Crear (my forever accountability buddy), Andrew Hyde, Jim Stephens, Kate Newburgh, Cynthia Banks, Bruce Uhrmacher, Norma Hafenstein, Cynthia Weiss, Lisa Henderson, Matt Mammola, Keren Nimmo, Scott Shrake, Liz Iraki, Matt Duncan, Kate Bailey, Pat Ranieri, Mary Wright, Sarah Case, Renee White Whitcomb, Adam Vicarel, Katie Richardson, Chelley Canales, Nancy Vahling, Erin Huizenga, and Erik Mitisek. And, a special shout out to Heather McGowan for her vision into the future of work, and Rita Irwin and Stephanie Springgay for their pioneering research on a/r/tography.

Bibliography

Abumrad, Jad. "Jad Abumrad: Accidental Scientist." Interview with Ophira Eisenberg, *Ask Me Another*, NPR, March 15, 2013. https://www.npr.org/2013/06/14/174123830/jad-abumrad-accidental-scientist.

Agarwal, Anant. "The Future Is Hybrid." *HuffPost*, March 9, 2017. http://www.huffingtonpost.com/entry/the-future-is-hybrid_us_58c081e6e4b0a797c1d398a4.

Bakhtin, Mikhail. "Discourse in the Novel." In *Literary Theory: An Anthology*, 2nd ed., edited by Julie Rivkin and Michael Ryan. New York: Wiley, 2004.

Berry, Barnett. *Teaching 2030: What We Must Do for Our Students and Our Public Schools—Now and in the Future.* New York: Teachers College Press, 2011.

Bessette, Chanelle. "10 Questions: Jennifer Hyman, Co-Founder and CEO, Rent the Runway." *Fortune*, August 19, 2014. https://fortune.com/2014/08/19/10-questions-jennifer-hyman-co-founder-and-ceo-rent-the-runway/.

Bhabha, Homi K. *The Location of Culture.* London: Routledge, 1994.

Bhabha, Homi K. "Culture's In-Between." In *Questions of Cultural Identity*, edited by Stuart Hall and Paul du Gay, 53–60. London: Sage, 1996.

Blanding, Michael. "The Business Case for Becoming a Jack-of-All-Trades." *Harvard Business School Working Knowledge*, January 14, 2020. https://hbswk.hbs.edu/item/the-business-case-for-becoming-a-jack-of-all-trades.

Brown, Bettina Lankard. "Changing Career Patterns." *ERIC Digest* no. 219 (October 2000): 1–6. https://files.eric.ed.gov/full-text/ED445235.pdf.

Brown, Brené. *The Gifts of Imperfection.* Center City, MN: Hazelden Publishing, 2010.

Browne, Irene, and Joya Misra. "The Intersection of Gender and Race in the Labor Market." *Annual Review of Sociology* 29 (August 2003): 487–513. https://doi.org/10.1146/annurev.soc.29.010202.100016.

Brubaker, Rogers, and Frederick Cooper. "Beyond "Identity." *Theory and Society* 29 (February 2000): 1–47. https://doi.org/10.1023/A:1007068714468.

Burguieres, Alexandra. "The Power of Voodoo, Times Two." *National Geographic,* June 25, 2008. https://www.natio-nalgeographic.com/travel/intelligent-travel/2008/06/25/the_power_of_voodoo_times_two/.

Carlos, Marjon. "This Downtown New York Baker Makes Working in the Kitchen Look Cooler Than Ever." *Vogue,* June 24, 2016. http://www.vogue.com/article/lexie-smith-new-york-baker-nine-to-five-dressing.

Carolina, Miranda A. "Q&A: A Salad Grows at the Getty Center: Artist Julia Sherman on the Roots of Her Unusual Project." *Los Angeles Times,* October 21, 2015. https://www.latimes.com/entertainment/arts/miranda/la-et-cam-salad-grows-at-getty-julia-sherman-20151020-column.html

Cheung, Alexia. "Bonding Over Bread (and Breakups)." *New York Times,* November 15, 2016. https://www.nytimes.com/2016/11/15/t-magazine/food/lexie-smith-lalo-res-taurant-georgia-hilmer.html.

Cho, Sumi, Kimberlé Williams Crenshaw, and Leslie McCall. "Toward a Field of Intersectionality Studies: Theory, Applications, and Praxis." *Signs* 38, no. 4 (summer 2013), 785–810. https://doi.org/10.1086/669608.

Cohan, Peter. "Why Hiring 'Rebel Talent' Is the Best Way to Grow Your Business, According to a Harvard Professor." *Inc.*, December 11, 2018. https://www.inc.com/peter-cohan/this-harvard-professor-says-hiring-rebels-will-grow-your-company-and-make-your-life-better.html.

Conner, Megan. "Iris Apfel: 'People Like Me Because I'm Different.'" *The Guardian,* July 19, 2015. https://www.theguardian.com/global/2015/jul/19/iris-apfel-interview-designer-fashion-film.

De Botton, Alain. "What's a Kinder Way to Frame Success?" Interview by Guy Raz, *TED Radio Hour,* NPR, November 1, 2013. https://www.npr.org/transcripts/240782763?storyId=240782763?storyId.

Dubnick, Randa. "Visible Poetry: Metaphor and Metonymy in the Paintings of René Magritte." *Contemporary Literature* 21, no. 3 (summer 1980), 407–19.

Easthope, Antony. "Bhabha, Hybridity, and Identity." *Textual Practice* 12, no. 2 (1998), 341–48. https://doi.org/10.1080/09502369808582312.

Epstein, David J. *Range: Why Generalists Triumph in a Specialized World.* New York: Riverhead Books, 2019.

Florida, Richard. *The Flight of the Creative Class: The New Global Competition for Talent.* New York: Harper Business, 2005.

Foucault, Michel. "Of Other Spaces, Utopias and Heterotopias." *Architecture, mouvement, continuité* (October 1984). http://web.mit.edu/allanmc/www/foucault1.pdf.

Foucault, Michel. "Translator's Introduction." In *This Is Not a Pipe*, translated by James Harkness, 1–12. Berkeley: University of California Press, 2008.

Gilbert, Dan. "When Do We Become the Final Version of Ourselves?" *TED Radio Hour*, NPR, June 19, 2015. https://www.npr.org/2015/06/19/414997263/when-do-we-become-the-final-version-of-ourselves.

Glassdoor Team. "Why 2016 Is the Year of the Hybrid Job." *Glassdoor*, March 22, 2016. https://www.glassdoor.com/blog/2016-year-hybrid-job/.

Goldsmith, Marshall. "Unleashing Your Many Identities." *Bloomberg*, June 23, 2007.

https://www.bloomberg.com/news/articles/2007-06-23/unleashing-your-many-identitiesbusinessweek-business-news-stock-market-and-financial-advice.

Goldsmith, Marshall. "My Dinner with Bono." *Marshall Goldsmith* (blog), July 6, 2015. https://www.linkedin.com/pulse/my-dinner-bono-marshall-goldsmith/.

Groom, Miriam. "Millennials, Individuality, and Digital Nomads: The New Employment Trends in 2017." *Recruiting Blogs*, December 21, 2016. https://recruitingblogs.com/profiles/blogs/millennials-individuality-and-digital-nomads-the-new-employment.

Hallett, Rachel, and Rosamund Hutt. "10 Jobs That Didn't Exist 10 Years Ago." *World Economic Forum*, June 7, 2016. https://www.weforum.org/agenda/2016/06/10-jobs-that-didn-t-exist-10-years-ago/.

Hamill, Kate. "'Monochromatic' Job Titles Are Becoming Obsolete, or: Embracing Being a Hybrid." *Freelancers Union*, September 17, 2014. https://blog.freelancersunion.org/2014/09/17/

monochromatic-job-titles-are-becoming-obsolete-or-em-bracing-being-hybrid/.

Hansen, Morten T. "IDEO CEO Tim Brown: T-Shaped Stars, the Backbone of IDEO's Collaborative Culture," *Chief Executive,* July 20, 2017. https://chiefexecutive.net/ideo-ceo-tim-brown-t-shaped-stars-the-backbone-of-ideoaes-collaborative-culture__trashed/.

Hislop, Christopher. "Gift Started It All for Singer-Songwriter Jennifer Kimball." *Fosters,* March 17, 2017. http://www.fosters.com/news/20170317/gift-started-it-all-for-singer-songwriter-jennifer-kimball.

Hubbell, Diana. "This NYC Artist's Radical Bread Is Baked to Be Destroyed." *Vice,* April 17, 2019. https://www.vice.com/en_us/article/bj9898/lexie-smiths-radical-bread-is-baked-to-be-destroyed.

Hyken, Shep. "The Gig Economy Opens the Door for Employment Opportunities." *Forbes,* August 1, 2018. https://www.forbes.com/sites/shephyken/2018/07/29/the-gig-economy-opens-the-door-for-employment-opportunities/#50e67e2f7662.

Illmind. "The Producer Who Created 'Beat Kits' Behind Today's Pop Music." Interview by Jacob Goldstein, *All Things Considered,* NPR, September 26, 2017. https://www.npr.org/2017/09/26/553799207/the-producer-who-created-beat-kits-behind-todays-pop-music.

Ing, David. "T-Shaped Professionals, T-Shaped Skills, Hybrid Managers." *Coevolving Innovations,* September 6, 2008. https://coevolving.com/blogs/index.php/archive/t-shaped-professionals-t-shaped-skills-hybrid-managers/.

Inkson, Kerr, and Michael B. Arthur. "How to Be a Successful Career Capitalist." *Organizational Dynamics* 30, no. 1 (June 2001) :48–61. https://doi.org/10.1016/S0090-2616(01)00040-7.

ILR School and the Aspen Institute Future of Work Initiative. "What Is a Gig Worker?" Gig Economy Data Hub, 2020. https://www.gigeconomydata.org/basics/what-gig-worker.

Irwin, Rita L., and Stephanie Springgay. "A/r/tography as Practice-Based Research." In *Arts Education and Curriculum Studies,* edited by Mindy R. Carter and Valerie Triggs, 162–78. New York: Routledge, 2017. https://doi.org/10.4324/9781315467016-17.

Johnson, Allan G. *Power, Privilege, and Difference,* 2nd ed. Boston: McGraw-Hill, 2006.

Kegan, Robert. *The Evolving Self: Problem and Process in Human Development.* Cambridge, MA: Harvard University Press, 1982.

Kegan, Robert. *In Over Our Heads: The Mental Demands of Modern Life.* Cambridge, MA: Harvard University Press, 1994.

Kim, Joshua. "What Might University HR Make of 'Rebel Talent?'" *Inside Higher Ed.*, January 21, 2019. https://www.insidehighered.com/blogs/technology-and-learning/what-might-university-hr-make-rebel-talent.

Lieber, Chavie. "The Nine Lives of Isaac Mizrahi." *Racked,* March 10, 2016. https://www.racked.com/2016/3/10/11183334/isaac-mizrahi-target-qvc.

Lynskey, Dorian. "U2: 'It's the Job of Art to be Divisive.'" *Guardian,* October 12, 2014. https://www.theguardian.com/music/2014/oct/12/u2-job-art-divisive-interview.

Malinga, Sibahle. "SA Must Get Ready for the Rise of Hybrid Jobs." *ITWeb,* November 1, 2019. https://www.itweb.co.za/content/KA3Wwqdl5bWqrydZ.

Manyika, James, Susan Lund, Michael Chui, Jacques Bughin, Jonathan Woetzel, Parul Batra, Ryan Ko, and Saurabh Sanghvi. "Jobs Lost, Jobs Gained: What the Future of Work Will Mean for Jobs, Skills, and Wages." McKinsey and Company, November 2017. https://www.mckinsey.com/featured-insights/future-of-work/jobs-lost-jobs-gained-what-the-future-of-work-will-mean-for-jobs-skills-and-wages.

McCall, Leslie. "The Complexity of Intersectionality." *Signs* 30, no. 3 (spring 2005), 1771–1800. https://doi.org/10.1086/426800.

McGowan, Heather E. "Future of Work: Heather E. McGowan." *YouTube*, May 10, 2018. https://www.youtube.com/watch?v=WOdds4RF3og.

Mitchell, Robert P. "Intersectionality: The Many Layers of an Individual." *Harvard Gazette,* October 31, 2016. http://news.harvard.edu/gazette/story/2016/10/intersectionality-the-many-layers-of-an-individual/.

Mizrahi, Isaac. "Fashion and Creativity." TED2008. Video, 13:58. http://www.ted.com/talks/isaac_mizrahi_on_fashion_and_creativity.html.

Newman, Judith. "Free to Be . . . Isaac Mizrahi." *New York Times,* August 28, 2013. http://www.nytimes.com/2013/08/29/fashion/free-to-be-isaac-mizrahi.html.

Newsroom. "Want to innovate? Look for rebel talents." *Morning Future,* June 10, 2019. https://www.morningfuture.com/en/article/2019/06/10/innovation-rebel-talent-francesca-gino/647.

Paquette, Danielle. "2018's Challenge: Too Many Jobs, Not Enough Workers." *Washington Post*, December 28, 2017. https://www.washingtonpost.com/news/wonk/wp/2017/12/28/2018s-challenge-too-many-jobs-not-enough-workers/?utm_term=.9aa85946c400.

Pearce, Kyle. "History's Greatest Geniuses: 7 Polymaths Who Changed the World." *DIY Genius,* September 2, 2019. https://www.diygenius.com/polymaths/.

Peirce, Neal, and Curtis Johnson. *Boundary Crossers: Community Leadership for a Global Age.* Academy of Leadership Press, 1997.

Pine, B. Joseph, and J. H. Gilmore. "The Experience Economy: Past, Present, and Future." In *Handbook on the Experience Economy,* edited by Jon Sundbo and Flemming Sørensen, 21–44. Northampton, MA: Edward Elgar, 2013. https://doi.org/10.4337/9781781004227.00007.

Pink, Daniel H. *Free Agent Nation: The Future of Working for Yourself.* Boston: Grand Central Publishing, 2001.

Pink, Daniel H. *A Whole New Mind.* New York: Riverhead Books, 2006.

Powell, Walter W., and Kaisa Snellman. "The Knowledge Economy." *Annual Review of Sociology* 30 (2004): 199–220. https://doi.org/10.1146/annurev.soc.29.010202.100037.

Ramirez, Cyndi. "Boss Babes: Meet Lexie Smith." *Taste the Style,* August 3, 2015. http://tastethestyle.com/boss-babes-meet-lexie-smith.

Roberts, Jeff John. "The Splinternet Is Growing." *Fortune,* May 29, 2019. https://fortune.com/2019/05/29/splinternet-online-censorship/.

Rodgers, Carol R., and Katherine H. Scott. "The Development of the Personal Self and Professional Identity in Learning to Teach." In *Handbook of Research on Teacher Education,* edited by Marilyn Cochran-Smith, Sharon Feiman-Nemser, D. John McIntyre, and Kelly E. Demers, 732–55. New York: Routledge, 2008.

Roetzer, Paul. "Hybrid Marketing Professionals: The Next Generation of Talent." *PR 20/20*, January 10, 2013. https://www.pr2020.com/blog/hybrid-marketing-professionals-the-next-generation-of-talent.

Rohn, Jennifer. "Leading a Double Life: Academics with Extraordinary Second Careers." *THE World University Ranking*, October 12, 2017. https://www.timeshighereducation.com/features/leading-double-life-academics-extraordinary-second-careers#survey-answer.

Rose, Todd. *The End of Average: How We Succeed in a World That Values Sameness*. London: Penguin Books, 2016.

Simmons, Gail. "Staying at the Top of Her Game." Interview with Veronica Dagher, *Secrets of Wealthy Women*, WSJ Podcasts, September 18, 2019. https://www.wsj.com/podcasts/secrets-of-wealthy-women.

Simmons, Michael. "How One Life Hack from a Self-Made Billionaire Leads to Exceptional Success." *Forbes*, March 23, 2015. https://www.forbes.com/sites/michaelsimmons/2015/03/23/how-one-life-hack-from-a-self-made-billionaire-leads-to-exceptional-success/#49b1337a543d.

Slaughter, Sam. "Your Job Title Is . . . What?" New York Times, October 23, 2015. https://www.nytimes.com/2015/10/25/fashion/your-job-title-is-what.html#

Slevin, Peter. *Michelle Obama: A Life*. New York: Vintage, 2015.

Stillman, Jessica. "Why It's Time to Embrace a 'Slash' Career." *Inc.*, September 25, 2014. https://www.inc.com/jessica-stillman/why-you-should-be-proud-to-be-a-slash.html

Tan, Chade-Meng. "The Story of Google Employee #107, a Jolly Good Fellow." *The Globe and Mail*, updated July 17, 2018. https://www.theglobeandmail.com/report-on-business/

careers/leadership-lab/the-story-of-google-employee-107-a-jolly-good-fellow/article29180302/.

Tan, Chade-Meng. "I'm Meng, Retired Jolly Good Fellow of Google. AMA!" *Tech in Asia*, May 16, 2016. https://www.techinasia. com/talk/chade-meng-tan-google-ama.

Van Meter, Jonathan. "Michelle Obama: A Candid Conversation with America's Champion and Mother in Chief." *Vogue*, November 11, 2016. http://www.vogue. com/13501355/michelle-obama-december-cover-interview-first-lady-white-house-departure/.

Werber, Cassie. "Michelle Obama's Career Advice: It's OK to Change Your Mind." *Quartz*, November 13, 2018. https://qz.com/work/1461671/michelle-obamas-career-advice-from-becoming/.

Wharton, University of Pennsylvania. "Running Faster, Falling Behind: John Hagel III on How American Business Can Catch Up." *Knowledge @ Wharton*, June 23, 2010. https://knowledge.wharton.upenn.edu/article/running-faster-falling-behind-john-hagel-iii-on-how-american-business-can-catch-up/.

Wilson, Chip. "Lululemon Athletica: Chip Wilson." Interview with Guy Raz, *How I Built This with Guy Raz*, NPR, June 18, 2018. https://www.npr.org/2018/06/14/620113439/lululemon-athletica-chip-wilson.

Zeller Jr., Tom. "Bono, Trying to Throw His Arms Around the World." *New York Times*, November 13, 2006. https://www.nytimes.com/2006/11/13/us/bono-trying-to-throw-his-arms-around-the-world.html.

About the Author

Dr. Sarabeth Berk is a hybrid professional who also researches hybrid professional identity. She's a TEDx speaker and was recognized by Colorado Inno as one of 50 "Inno on Fire" recipients, people who are doing incredibly innovative work. Sarabeth calls herself a creative disruptor because she blends her artist/researcher/educator/designer identities to lead and create innovation strategies that radically connect resources and people in new ways.

After Sarabeth underwent her own professional identity crisis, she learned she was a hybrid and that concept revolutionized her career path. Now, she's obsessed with changing the way we see the workforce and helping professionals realize that their unique value lies at the intersections of their multiple identities.

Berk obtained her PhD in curriculum studies and teaching from the University of Denver, and has degrees from the School of the Art Institute of Chicago and Rhode Island School of Design. Her background includes leading innovation and entrepreneurship initiatives in K–12, higher education, and community programs. She often mentors startups that are building social impact ventures. Berk is also a member of the Denver County Cultural Council, and she loves to mountain bike, ski, travel, do word puzzles, and get lost in nature.

CPSIA information can be obtained
at www.ICGtesting.com
Printed in the USA
LVHW050713150322
713413LV00021B/3086